RSPB
RESERVES VISITING

edited by Anthony Chapman

Published by the Royal Society for the Protection of Birds, The Lodge, Sandy, Bedfordshire SG19 2DL.

Great care has been taken throughout this book to ensure accuracy, but the Society cannot accept any responsibility for any error that may occur.

Cover symbol: Crown copyright, reproduced with the permission of the Controller of Her Majesty's Stationery Office.

Maps: Hilary Welch
Design: Martine Blaney
Illustrations: John Busby
Typesetting: Bedford Typesetters Limited
Printing and binding: David Green Printers Ltd.
Distribution: Christopher Helm (Publishers) Ltd.

ISBN No 0 903138 24 7

Contents

Introduction

With some 120 reserves in its care, the Royal Society for the Protection of Birds owns more than 100 square miles of some of the United Kingdom's finest bird habitats, and manages a further 100 square miles through the kind co-operation and agreement of landowners.

Most of our reserves are open to visitors (and others will be opened when they are ready for them), enabling thousands of people to enjoy watching some of our rarest and most spectacular birds and other wildlife, and to savour the peace and tranquillity of beautiful scenery.

The RSPB's reserves have been established over a period of more than 50 years through the purchase and leasing of suitable land as well as the bequests and gifts of well-wishers. The massive contribution of funds by our members, statutory grant-aiding bodies, charitable trusts and the World Wildlife Fund has enabled more land to be safeguarded for wild birds than would otherwise have been possible. With increasing demands on our land, the RSPB's reserves are becoming ever more precious. If you are not a member of the Society, we hope you will want to join to support our campaign to protect Britain's birds.

Ian Prestt, CBE
Director General
RSPB

Visiting RSPB Reserves

The Royal Society for the Protection of Birds has a long tradition of establishing nature reserves, starting with the bird sanctuaries of pre-war years and building up to the present total of 120 reserves which are located throughout the United Kingdom. A large body of reserve wardens, backed up by a team of managers, land agents and ecologists, ensure that the RSPB's land-holding is managed to the best advantage of wild bird populations and other native wildlife. The Society's accumulated experience in practical habitat management for nature conservation is second to none.

In fulfilment of the objective, expressed by the Society's Royal Charter, of 'developing a public interest in wild birds and their place in nature', most of our reserves have the facilities to enable a lot of visitors to enjoy them for their scenery, their pleasant walks and, above all, their exciting variety of wild birds. RSPB reserve habitats range from rolling moorland to wide estuaries, from spectacular sea-cliffs to quiet marshes and from broadleaved woodlands to precious heaths.

Our policy is to encourage RSPB and Young Ornithologists' Club members, as well as the general public, to visit our reserves, subject only to the restrictions that must be applied to fulfil their main purpose – to provide rich and undisturbed places for wild birds to use for nesting, feeding, roosting and as resting-places on migration. Other scientific features must also be conserved with care.

By providing wardening, both paid and voluntary, and installing nature trails and waymarked paths, boardwalks, observation hides and information centres, we can reconcile the twin objectives of bird conservation and showing birds to people – a special technique that the RSPB has developed over two decades of imaginative reserve management.

This guide has been produced with the aim of helping more people to enjoy the reserves whose survival depends on the support of over half a million RSPB and YOC members as well as the goodwill of all those who visit them.

We hope that you will enjoy visiting many of these RSPB reserves.

Enquiries

RSPB offices to which enquiries should be made:

Reserves Division, The Royal Society for the Protection of Birds, The Lodge, Sandy, Bedfordshire SG19 2DL (tel: 0767 80551).

RSPB Scottish Office, 17 Regent Terrace, Edinburgh EH7 5BN (tel: 031 556 5624).

RSPB Wales Office, Bryn Isel, The Bank, Newtown, Powys ZY16 2AB (tel: 0686 26678).

RSPB Orkney Officer, Smyril, Stenness, Stromness KW16 3JX (tel: 0856 850176).

RSPB Shetland Officer, Seaview, Sandwick ZE2 9HP (tel: 095 05 506).

Balranald

Loch Gruinart

Rathlin Island Cliffs

Lough Foyle

Castlecaldwell
Forest

Shanes Castle

Green Island &
Greencastle Point

Grassholm

50 km

50 miles

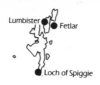

Visiting Arrangements

The arrangements for visiting each of the reserves described in this guide are expected to remain, but the RSPB reserves the right to modify them if necessary. The current arrangements for each year are given in a free *Reserves Visiting leaflet* which is issued to members with the winter issue of the Society's quarterly magazine *Birds*, or is obtainable free from RSPB headquarters. Visitor facilities are being improved year by year.

All visitors to our reserves are asked to observe the following **standard rules**:

● In many places only *part* of the reserve is open to visitors, the remainder being kept quiet for the wildlife or for management reasons. Information Centres, shops and in some cases hides and toilets, are *not necessarily* open all the hours that the particular reserve is.

● **Entry charges** (where indicated) are incurred by non-members only, and children are admitted half-price. Members of the RSPB and YOC (including those covered by supplements) are admitted *free* on production of their *membership cards*. We regret that charges cannot be refunded.

● **Coach parties and groups of ten or more people** must arrange their visit well in advance by writing (enclosing a stamped addressed envelope) to the warden, who may be able to escort them.

● **Dogs** may not be taken into the reserves.

● Visitors may encounter management necessarily being undertaken in part of the reserve which may involve temporary disturbance to the birds. We regret any inconvenience that may be caused in these circumstances.

General enquiries to the Reserves Division, RSPB, The Lodge, Sandy, Bedfordshire SG19 2DL (tel: 0767 80551).

Practical Points for Visitors

 Look for this sign! Starting in 1987, special RSPB **Direction Signs** will be erected over a period of time throughout the country to guide travellers to the reserves.

 Shading indicates the **Reserve Area**, but in some cases it has not been possible to include the entire holding on these maps.

 The directions under **Location**, coupled with the map are intended to guide visitors, with the aid of an OS map or road atlas, to the **Reserve Entrance** or other access points. The national six-figure grid reference usually refers to that point.

P Reserve (or nearby) **Car Park**. The words 'car parking' indicate informal and limited space for parking such as in a lay-by.

 Some facilities for **Disabled Visitors**. We try to make it possible for disabled people to visit and enjoy our reserves for birdwatching wherever practicable. In many instances hides have been adapted for wheelchair access and in others special paths and boardwalks have been installed. A *free* leaflet with further details of disabled access is available from the Reserves Division.

 Visitors are referred to the local **Tourist Information Centre**, which can advise about local accommodation, bus and rail services etc. The larger ones can book accommodation for visitors. The Society does not maintain details of accommodation near the reserves (with a few exceptions that are listed – although this does not imply any recommendation). In addition to the advertisers here, a large number of hotels, guest houses and bed and breakfast addresses near to RSPB reserves advertise in *Birds*, the Society's membership magazine.

IC Many reserves are equipped with some form of **Information Centre**, ranging from Nature Centres, with their teaching facilities and shops, to outdoor shelters with identification displays and basic reserve guidance. *Please note* that these buildings are not necessarily open all the hours that the particular reserve is.

G   **Guide** A series of illustrated leaflets or booklets, describing individual reserves more fully are for sale on reserves or by post (adding 20p to the price indicated) from RSPB headquarters.

S   Several reserves have a **Shop** that sells items from the RSPB gift catalogue.

WC   **Toilets** are available on or beside the reserve.

Public Transport For those who choose to visit our reserves by public transport, the nearest British Rail station is listed in each case. Occasionally the station is within walking distance, but usually a bus or taxi will be needed to complete the journey to the reserve.

Clothing and Footwear Visitors are advised to wear or carry warm and waterproof garments because the weather on reserves, particularly those in upland or exposed situations, can be inclement, even in summer. Visitor paths are often uneven, sometimes rugged, so stout shoes or boots should be worn. Wellingtons are advisable for wet habitats like the marshes.

Wardens Bearing in mind their other duties, wardens or their assistants are pleased to answer written enquiries and to advise visitors on arrival as to where to go and which birds are about. Please note the requirement under *Standard Rules* for group visits.

Nature trails Some are interpreted with leaflets, others with path-side display boards. In other cases, simple **waymarked paths** are provided.

Additional Notes

Tenure The RSPB either owns the land for its reserves or leases it from one or more owners. Sometimes the reserve is established by management agreement with the owner. Reserves are being extended all the time, so the acreage and boundary indicated may not be up-to-date in each case.

Status A Site of Special Scientific Interest (**SSSI**) is land which is officially classified by the Nature Conservancy Council as being of particular importance for nature conservation, under the provisions of the Wildlife and Countryside Act, 1981. (A different system operates in Northern Ireland.) Grades 1 or 2 refer to those sites which are listed in *A Nature Conservation Review* – the NCC's inventory of élite nature conservation land in Britain. An asterisk indicates that a site has international importance.

Birds The information is necessarily brief and selective but is intended to convey the ornithological 'flavour' of each reserve during the breeding season and at other times of the year. All the species mentioned will not necessarily be present during a particular visit.

Other Wildlife A few notable species of flora and fauna which may be encountered by the visitor are given to enhance the interest of the reserve.

How to
see more birds

"When I was warden on the Ouse Washes I would often be sitting in the hide quietly watching the ducks feeding nearby. Then a coach or group of cars would arrive in the car park. As the bird-watchers disgorge from the vehicles, all chatting away, the ducks start to swim gently out from the bankside away from the hides. The birdwatchers come along the path and noisily cross the bridge over the river; the ducks swim faster. Finally, the visitors stamp up the steps and the straggling ducks take off. So by the time the watchers are in the hides there are no ducks nearer than half a mile. Then there is always the chap who, because the hide is crammed with people, has to stand on top of the bank silhouetted against the fine fenland sky! That is the last straw for the ducks: they go, and they have 20 miles to choose from."

Jeremy Sorensen, RSPB Warden
(*Birds* magazine, 1983)

The lesson is obvious: be quiet, careful and inconspicuous. Choose subdued colours for clothes and wear a hat of some sort — to disguise head shape. Walk quietly and slowly, do not talk loudly, make use of cover such as banks, trees and bushes. Avoid the skyline and try to keep the light behind you. In many areas, especially woodland, it pays to find a sheltered spot, perhaps on the edge of a clearing or ride, sit still and let the birds come to you.

When watching birds at sea, choose a time of day when the sun is behind you. Pick a viewpoint that juts out over the sea: about 20-30 feet above sea level. Remember that birds sitting on the water are in the valleys of the swell most of the time, so pan very slowly to give yourself a good chance of seeing them.

In a hide, to avoid disturbing the birds, open and close doors and windows quietly; close the flaps before you leave; do not put your hands or binoculars through the viewing holes.

Birdwatchers' Code of Conduct

Today's birdwatchers are a powerful force for nature conservation. The number of those of us interested in birds rises continually and it is vital that we take seriously our responsibility to avoid any harm to birds. We must also present a responsible image to non-birdwatchers who may be affected by our activities and particularly those on whose sympathy and support the future of birds may rest.

There are 10 points to bear in mind:

1. The welfare of birds must come first.

2. Habitat must be protected.

3. Keep disturbance to birds and their habitat to a minimum.

4. When you find a rare bird think carefully about whom you should tell.

5. Do not harass rare migrants.

6. Abide by the bird protection laws at all times.

7. Respect the rights of landowners.

8. Respect the rights of other people in the countryside.

9. Make your records available to the local bird recorder.

10. Behave abroad as you would when birdwatching at home.

Industrial Landscape

All too often, industrial progress has led to environmental reverses. But not always; fortunately for our countryside and wildlife, British Gas has shown consistent concern for the environment during nearly two decades of unparalleled growth.

Since natural gas first came ashore from the North Sea, British Gas has constructed a national network of unseen, underground mains, thousands of miles long. It has sited and landscaped the various installations needed to provide an efficient and reliable gas supply to over 16 million customers to harmonise with the rural environment. Some of these installations are so acceptable to nature that they have become, in effect, small nature reserves, inhabited by the most unexpected flora and fauna.

And, most recently, the development of underground gas storage in salt cavities, and undersea storage in the revolutionary Rough Field project have helped to make the process of gas supply more economic and even more unobtrusive.

Why do the gas people show so much concern for the countryside? Because the relationship between British Gas and the community isn't just a commercial one – it depends on mutual goodwill. That's one of the reasons why we put a lot of energy into dealing with our social responsibilities. But then, energy is our business.

British Gas
ENERGY IS OUR BUSINESS

ENGLAND

Adur Estuary, West Sussex

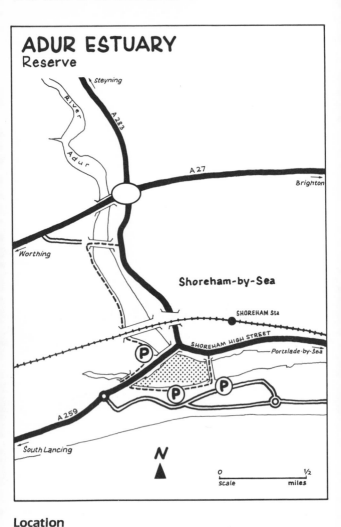

ADUR ESTUARY
Reserve

Steyning

River

A 283

Adur

A 27

Brighton

Worthing

Shoreham-by-Sea

SHOREHAM Sta

SHOREHAM HIGH STREET

Portslade-by-Sea

A 259

South Lancing

N

0 ½
scale miles

Location
Occupying a portion of the tidal River Adur within Shoreham-by-Sea, the reserve may be viewed from the south side between the footbridge from the town centre and the A259 Norfolk Bridge.

Tenure
25 acres owned.

Status
SSSI.

Warden
None present. Enquiries to RSPB South-east Regional Office, Scan House, 4 Church Street, Shoreham-by-Sea BN4 5DQ (tel: 0273 463642).

Habitat
Inter-tidal mudflats and saltmarsh.

Birds
Redshank, ringed plover and dunlin feed in winter on the mud, roosting at high tides on the nearby airfield. Avocet, bar-tailed godwit, curlew, whimbrel, knot and shelduck are occasionally seen. Several gull species occur including rare sightings of the Mediterranean gull.

Other wildlife
Sea purslane, glasswort and sea aster are some of the saltwater plants.

Visiting
Good views may be obtained of the river from adjacent footpaths near Shoreham High Street. An illustrated leaflet *River Adur Wildlife Walk* is available (price 20p) from the RSPB South-east Office (above). There is a car park at the edge of the recreation ground by Norfolk Bridge (TQ/211050).

Facilities
P

86 High Street, Shoreham-by-Sea, West Sussex (tel: 079 17 2086).

Nearest railway station
Shoreham (¼ mile) on the line from London (Victoria) to Portsmouth.

Arne, Dorset

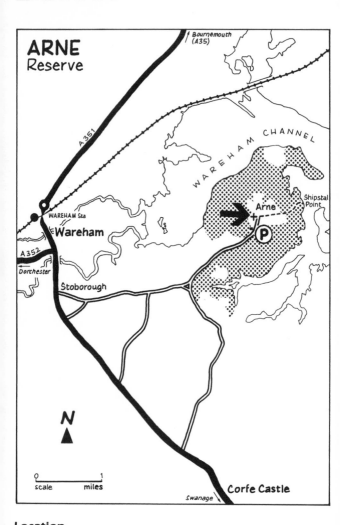

Location
The Arne peninsular lies in Poole Harbour east of Wareham, and the reserve is approached off the A351 road to Swanage, ½ mile from Wareham, turning as signposted in Stoborough. SY/972877.

Tenure
1,312 acres, mostly owned.

Status
SSSI. Grade 1*.

Warden
Bryan Pickess, Syldata, Arne, Wareham BH20 5BJ.

Habitat
Extensive heathland of heather, gorse clumps and scattered pines with some valley bogs. Also mixed woodland, fen with reedbeds and creeks with saltmarsh on the edge of Poole Harbour.

Birds
Dartford warbler, nightjar and stonechat breed on the heaths, and sparrowhawk and woodpeckers in the woods. Large flocks of black-tailed godwit and spotted redshank use the foreshore during migration. Wintering species include red-breasted merganser, goldeneye, wigeon and hen harrier.

Other wildlife
Roe and sika deer, all six species of British reptiles including sand lizard and smooth snake, and 22 species of dragonflies which favour the bogs and pools are part of Arne's rich fauna.

Visiting
The Shipstal part of the reserve is open at all times, the rest of the reserve being closed except to parties by prior arrangement with the warden. The reserve car park, with toilets, is situated in Arne village and the public bridleway to Shipstal, with its nature trail and leaflet, starts opposite the church. Visitors are expected to keep to the paths and trackways, except on the beach.

Facilities
P **WC** **G** 30p

The Whitehouse, Shore Road, Swanage (tel: 0929 422885).

See advertisements page 24.

Nearest railway station
Wareham on the main line from London with connecting bus service through Stoborough (4 miles).

Dartford warbler

Aylesbeare Common
Devon

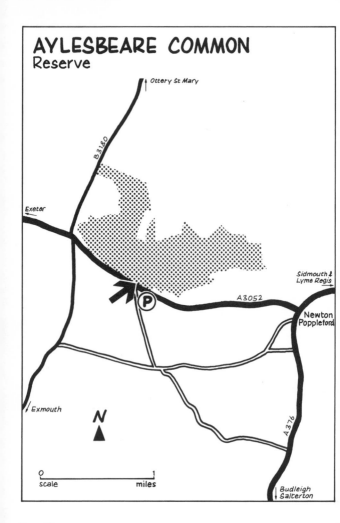

AYLESBEARE COMMON
Reserve

Ottery St Mary

B3180

Exeter

Sidmouth & Lyme Regis

A3052

Newton Poppleford

Exmouth

N

A376

scale   0   1   miles

Budleigh Salterton

Location
Comprising part of the Pebblebed Commons of south Devon, the reserve lies to the north of the A3052 Lyme Regis to Exeter road one mile west of Newton Poppleford. SY/057898.

Tenure
450 acres leased from the Clinton Devon Estates.

Status
SSSI. Grade 1.

Warden
Present from April to August, c/o The Post Office, Newton Poppleford, near Sidmouth, Devon.

Habitat
Both dry and wet heathland with valley bogs, streams, some woodland and alder scrub.

Birds
Nightjar, stonechat, yellowhammer and curlew breed on the heath, with tree pipit on the edge of and marsh tit in the woodland.

Other wildlife
Plants include dwarf gorse, pink butterwort, bog pimpernel and royal fern. Roe deer, wood cricket, adder and many dragonfly species occur.

Visiting
Access at all times, but visitors are asked to keep to the footpaths and firebreak paths from which good views of the reserve are obtained. A waymarked trail starts across the road from the public car park.

Facilities
P

Silver Street, Ottery St Mary, Devon (tel: 040 481 3964).

See advertisements pages 24, 44.

Nearest railway station
Exeter on the main line from London. A bus service to Sidmouth passes the reserve.

Roe deer

Barfold Copse, Surrey

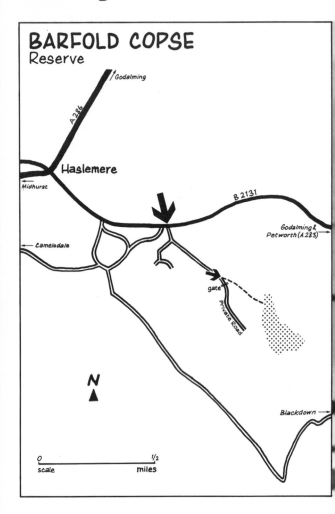

Location
Off the B2131 road to Petworth ½ mile east of Haslemere. Park by the *second* turning to Black Down and follow the public footpath then track to the reserve. SU/914324.

Tenure
13 acres owned.

Warden
None present. Enquiries to RSPB Reserves Division.

Habitat
Deciduous woodland of oak, ash and birch with old hazel coppice, being part of a larger wooded area.

Birds
The common woodland species including tits, robin and nuthatch nest in the wood.

Other wildlife
The golden-banded dragonfly is often seen and white admiral butterflies are usual. Wild daffodil, golden-scaled fern and pendulous sedge are among the plants.

Visiting
Access at all times along the woodland paths. Visitors should keep clear of the derelict buildings.

The Library, 27 The Square, Petersfield, Hampshire (tel: 0730 63451).

Nearest railway station
Haslemere (1 mile) on the main line from London (Waterloo) to Portsmouth.

Redpoll

Bempton Cliffs, Humberside

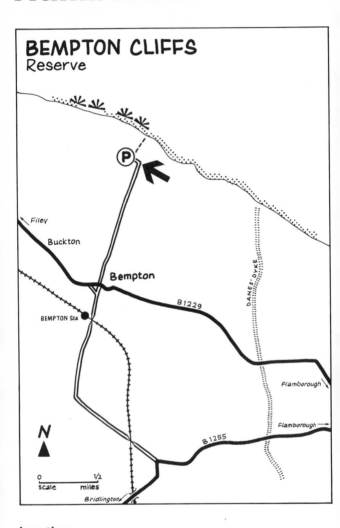

BEMPTON CLIFFS
Reserve

Filey

Buckton

Bempton

BEMPTON Sta

B1229

DANES' DYKE

Flamborough

Flamborough

B 1255

Bridlington

N

0   1/2
scale   miles

Location
Part of the spectacular chalk cliffs that stretch from Flamborough Head to Speeton, the reserve is approached up the cliff road from Bempton village which is on the B1229 from Flamborough, near Bridlington, to Filey. TA/197738.

Tenure
Lengths of cliff totalling three miles are owned.

Status
SSSI. Grade 1*.

Warden
Present from April to August, c/o The Post Office, Bempton, near Bridlington, Humberside.

Habitat
Chalk cliffs with numerous cracks and ledges, rising to 400ft in places, and topped by a clay soil with grass and scrub.

Birds
Enormous numbers of seabirds nest on the cliffs, including thousands of guillemots, razorbills, puffins, kittiwakes, fulmars, herring gulls and several pairs of shags at the boulder base. Here the only gannetry on the mainland of Britain is growing annually, with 650 pairs in 1986. Many migrants pass offshore, including terns, skuas and shearwaters, while species such as wheatear, ring ouzel, merlin and bluethroat frequent the cliff-top on migration.

Visiting
Access at all times to the cliff-top path on which are sited four safe observation barriers (one on a neighbour's land), providing excellent views of the seabird colonies including the gannetry. Visitors *must* keep to the footpath and observation points because the cliffs are dangerous.

Facilities
P IC ♿ G 50p

Prince Street, Bridlington, Humberside (tel: 0262 673474).

See advertisements pages 24 and 25.

Nearest railway station
Bempton (1½ miles) on the line from Hull to Scarborough.

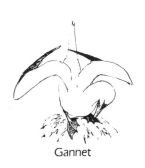

Gannet

Blacktoft Sands, Humberside

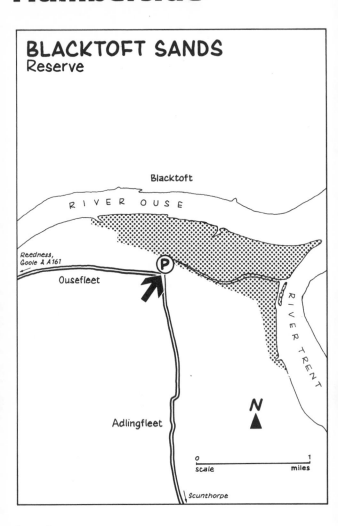

BLACKTOFT SANDS
Reserve

Blacktoft

R I V E R   O U S E

Reedness,
Goole & A161

Ousefleet

P

R I V E R   T R E N T

N

Adlingfleet

0   1
scale   miles

Scunthorpe

Location
Situated at the confluence of the rivers Ouse and Trent on the inner Humber estuary, the reserve is reached from the A161 road east of Goole through Reedness and Ousefleet. SE/843232.

Tenure
460 acres leased from Associated British Ports.

Status
SSSI. Grade 1*.

Warden
Andrew Grieve, Hillcrest, High Street, Whitgift, Goole DN14 8HL.

Habitat
A large tidal reedbed, fringed by saltmarsh, with an area of shallow, brackish water lagoons created by management.

Birds
Redshank, shoveler, gadwall, pochard and little ringed plover nest on the lagoons which are visited by many species of waders on passage — avocet, stints, greenshank, godwits, sandpipers and occasional rarities. The reedbeds contain reed warbler, bearded tit and water rail and a pair of marsh harriers has occasionally nested in them. Short-eared owl, hen harrier and merlin visit in winter, as do many wildfowl.

Other wildlife
Water vole and fox are present.

Visiting
Open on all days *except Tuesday*, 9.00am to 9.00pm or sunset when earlier. £2 charge for non-members. Five hides overlook the lagoons and reeds and are approached from the car park and picnic site by firm paths.

Facilities
P   WC   IC **G** 30p

Goole Library, Carlisle Street, Goole, Humberside (tel: 0405 2187).

Nearest railway station
Goole (8 miles) on the line from Doncaster to Hull.

Hen harrier

Chapel Wood, Devon

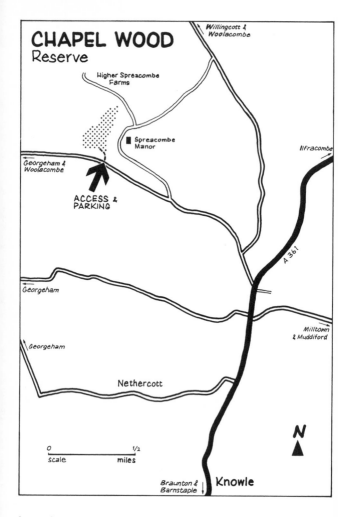

Location
Situated near the north Devon coast, this reserve is approached from the A361 Barnstaple to Ilfracombe road, turning to Spreacombe two miles north of Braunton. SS/483413.

Tenure
14 acres owned.

Honorary warden
Cyril Manning, 8 Chichester Park, Woolacombe, North Devon.

Habitat
A valley woodland with a variety of tree species.

Birds
Nuthatch, treecreeper, redstart, pied and spotted flycatchers, all three species of woodpeckers and occasionally raven and buzzard nest on or near the reserve.

Visiting
The reserve may be visited at any time by obtaining a permit by post from the honorary warden (enclosing SAE). Cars should be parked on the verge near the entrance stile from which visitors cross a field to the reserve gate with the RSPB sign. The gates must be closed. A path, with several branches, encircles the wood.

20 Holland Street, Barnstaple, Devon (tel: 0271 72742).

See advertisement page 44.

Nearest railway station
Barnstaple (10 miles) on the line from Exeter.

Pied flycatcher

Church Wood, Buckinghamshire

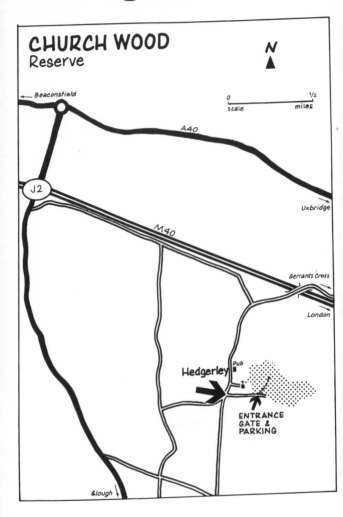

CHURCH WOOD Reserve

N

Beaconsfield

A40

J2

Uxbridge

M40

Gerrards Cross

London

Hedgerley Pub

ENTRANCE GATE & PARKING

Slough

0 .... ½
scale   miles

Location
Situated beside the Chilterns village of Hedgerley which is reached from the M40 or A40 intersections near Beaconsfield, turning south on the A355 road to Slough. Immediately south of the M40 turn left for Hedgerley village where a private track to the reserve is entered beside the pond beyond the pub. SU/968873.

Tenure
34 acres owned.

Warden
None present. Enquiries to Reserves Division.

Habitat
Mixed woodland with mature beech, ash and oak as well as birch, alder and hazel coppice, forming part of the more extensive Chiltern woods.

Birds
Nuthatch, the three species of woodpeckers, stock dove, blackcap and several species of tits nest in this woodland.

Other wildlife
Fox and muntjac deer occur as do both white admiral and purple hairstreak butterflies. Butcher's broom and green helleborine are interesting plants.

Visiting
Access at all times along waymarked paths which encircle the wood. Visitors are asked to park *beside* the track to the field gate and entrance to avoid impeding farm traffic.

Central Library, St Ive's Road, Maidenhead, Berkshire (tel: 0628 781110).

Nearest railway station
Gerrards Cross (4 miles) on the line from London (Marylebone).

Lesser spotted woodpecker

Church Wood, Blean, Kent

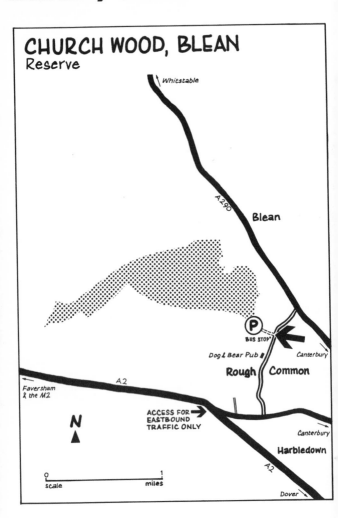

CHURCH WOOD, BLEAN
Reserve

Whitstable

A290

Blean

P
BUS STOP

Dog & Bear Pub

Canterbury

Rough Common

A2

Faversham & the M2

ACCESS FOR EASTBOUND TRAFFIC ONLY

N

Canterbury

Harbledown

A2

Dover

0 scale 1 miles

Location

Part of the extensive Blean Forest on the west of Canterbury, Church Wood is entered at Rough Common. Approaching from the west on the A2, take the first road on the left signposted Canterbury then the second turning on the left signposted Rough Common. After ½ mile, pass a pub on the left then turn left after a further 200 yards (by bus stop). Follow stone track for 500 yards to the reserve car park. TR/126593.

Tenure

440 acres owned.

Status
SSSI. Grade 1.

Warden
Michael Walter, 11 Garden Close, Rough Common, Canterbury CT2 9BP.

Habitat
Mainly deciduous woodland on sandy soil, being part of a larger block of some 2,000 acres. Mature oakwood contrasts with open sweet chestnut coppice and areas of silver birch, and is crossed by several rides.

Birds
Green, great spotted and lesser spotted woodpeckers, nightingale, tree pipit, willow warbler, blackcap, garden warbler and nuthatch are some of the breeding species, and notably redstart, hawfinch and wood warbler which are scarce in south-east England. Crossbills occur regularly.

Other wildlife
One of the few sites of Britain's most endangered butterfly, the heath fritillary, whose caterpillars feed on the yellow cow-wheat and whose numbers are being increased by habitat management. The butterflies fly on sunny days from mid-June to late July.

Visiting
Access at all times along three waymarked paths of one, two and three miles length respectively. Visitors should keep to these paths.

Facilities
P

13 Longmarket, Canterbury, Kent (tel: 0227 66567).

Nearest railway station
Canterbury (2 miles) on the main line from London (Victoria).

Wood warbler

Churnet Valley Woods, Staffs.

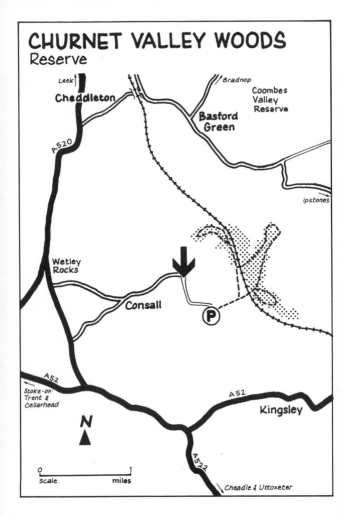

CHURNET VALLEY WOODS
Reserve

Leek
Cheddleton
Bradnop
Coombes Valley Reserve
Basford Green
A520
Ipstones
Wetley Rocks
Consall
P
Stoke-on-Trent & Cellarhead
A52
A52
Kingsley
N
0 Scale 1 miles
A522
Cheadle & Uttoxeter

Location

Lying in the steep-sided valley of the River Churnet, the three properties of Chase Wood, Rough Knipe and Booths Wood are entered down the minor road from Consall village, east of the A522 from Cheadle to Leek. SS/990489.

Tenure

183 acres owned.

Warden

Maurice Waterhouse, Coombes Valley Reserve (see page 40).

Habitat

Mature broadleaved woodland clothing the valley slopes rises to 200ft above the river and canal and contains oak, ash, wych elm, rowan, bird cherry, guelder rose and hazel.

Birds

The resident species of nuthatch, treecreeper, sparrowhawk, tits and woodpeckers are joined in summer by numerous garden warblers, blackcaps, willow warblers, wood warblers and red-starts with several pairs of whitethroat, lesser whitethroat and pied flycatcher. Siskins and redpolls occur in winter.

Other wildlife

Giant bellflower, broad-leaved helleborine and wild garlic flower in the woodland where white-letter hairstreak butterflies may be seen. Grass snakes are common.

Visiting

Access at all times *on foot* from the new Country Park car park off the private road (SJ/995483). Visitors should walk downhill to the canal bridge where waymarked paths enter the three woods for circular walks.

Facilities
P

New Stockwell House, Stockwell Street, Leek, Staffs (tel: 0538 385181).

Nearest railway station

Stoke-on-Trent (13 miles) on the main line from Birmingham New Street.

Sparrowhawk

Coombes Valley, Staffordshire

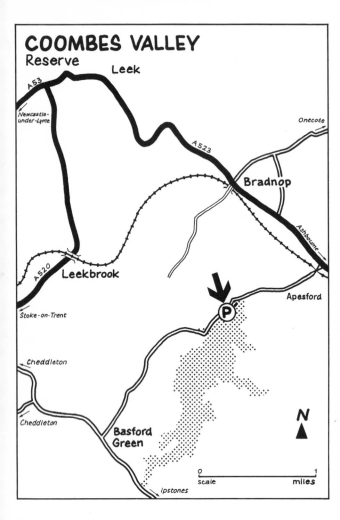

COOMBES VALLEY
Reserve
Leek
A 53
Newcastle-under-Lyme
Onecote
A 523
Bradnop
Ashbourne
A 520
Leekbrook
Stoke-on-Trent
Apesford
P
Cheddleton
Cheddleton
Basford Green
N
Ipstones
0   scale   1   miles

Location
This secluded valley lies off the A523 road to Ashbourne, three miles south-east of Leek. Turn up the minor road to Apesford (as signposted) and the reserve is entered after one mile. SK/009534.

Tenure
263 acres owned.

Status
SSSI.

Warden
Maurice Waterhouse, Six Oaks Farm, Bradnop, Leek ST13 7EU.

Habitat
A steep-sided valley with a rocky stream and slopes covered by oak woodland, bracken clearings and pasture.

Birds
Redstart, wood warbler and pied flycatcher typify the breeding birds' community which also contains tree pipit, sparrowhawk, tawny and long-eared owls and the three species of woodpeckers. Dipper, grey wagtail and kingfisher frequent the stream. Large flocks of fieldfare, redwing, tits and finches occur in winter.

Other wildlife
A fine site for badgers which breed in several setts. There is a rich beetle fauna. Several orchid species occur.

Visiting
Open on all days *except Tuesday*, 9.00am to 9.00pm or sunset when earlier. A nature trail with leaflet explores the reserve where there are two hides, one overlooking the stream and pond and another elevated in the tree canopy.

Facilities
P   **WC**   **IC**   **G** 30p

New Stockwell House, Stockwell Street, Leek, Staffs (tel: 0538 385181).

Nearest railway station
Stoke-on-Trent (13 miles) on the main line from Birmingham New Street.

Badger

Coquet Island, Northumberland

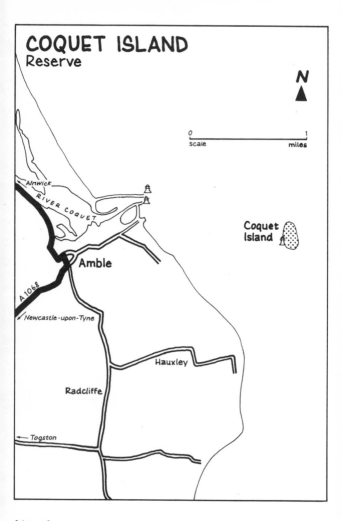

Location
Lying one mile off the Northumberland coast near the village of Amble, this small island may not be visited to avoid disturbing the seabirds. However, a boat trip around it provides good views of the nesting colonies. NU/294046.

Tenure
16 acres leased from the Northumberland Estates.

Status
SSSI. Grade 2.

Warden
Present from April to August, c/o The Post Office, Amble, near Morpeth, Northumberland.

Habitat
A low, flat-topped island with rocky and shingle shores.

Birds
Large colonies of Sandwich, common and Arctic terns nest on the open island as well as several pairs of the scarce roseate tern. Hundreds of puffins breed in turf burrows and there is also a thriving colony of eider ducks.

Other wildlife
Grey seals, which nest on the Farne Islands to the north, may be seen around the island.

Visiting
Boat trips around the island can be arranged, weather and tidal conditions permitting, with the boatman, Gordon Easton (tel: 0665 710384 or 712460).

The Shambles, Northumberland Hall, Alnwick, Northumberland (tel: 0665 603129).

Nearest railway station
Acklington (5 miles) on the main line from Newcastle to Berwick.

Common tern

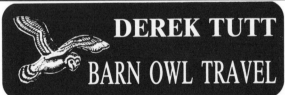

Dungeness, Kent

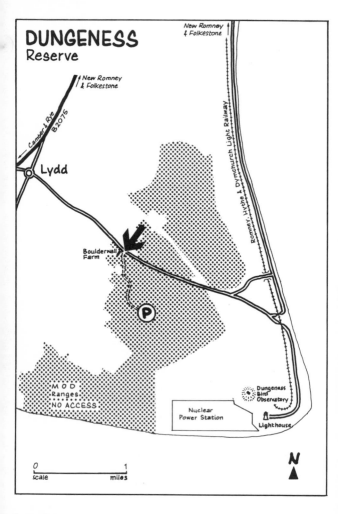

Location
Situated on the large and exposed shingle foreland of Dungeness, the reserve is entered off the straight Lydd to Dungeness road as signposted. TR/063196.

Tenure
1,260 acres owned with 769 acres leased from Folkestone Water Company.

Status
SSSI. Grade 1*.

Warden

Peter Makepeace, Boulderwall Farm, Dungeness Road, Lydd, Romney Marsh, TN29 9PN.

Habitat

Extensive shingle, part of which has been excavated to form flooded pits of high value to waterfowl. Also natural ponds, marshy depressions and scattered clumps of gorse and bramble.

Birds

The islands of Burrowes Pit have a large nesting colony of common and Sandwich terns with black-headed gulls and a few pairs of the rare Mediterranean gull. Wheatear, great and little grebes also nest. Large flocks of teal, shoveler, mallard, pochard and tufted duck occur outside the breeding season, other winter visitors being goldeneye, goosander, smew and both Slavonian and red-necked grebes. Dungeness is a famous landfall for small migrants including many rarities.

Other wildlife

The introduced marsh frog is abundant. Viper's bugloss and Nottingham catchfly flower on the shingle.

Visiting

Open on all days *except Tuesday*, 9.00am to 9.00pm or sunset when earlier. £2 charge for non-members. Three hides overlook the Burrowes Pit and there is also a waymarked path of 1 ½ miles length.

Facilities

P   **WC**   **IC**   ♿   **G** 30p

2 Littlestone Road, New Romney, Kent (tel: 0679 64044).

See advertisement page 44.

Nearest railway station

Rye (10 miles) on the line from Ashford to Hastings. A light railway travels from Hythe to Dungeness.

Little grebe

Eastwood,
Greater Manchester

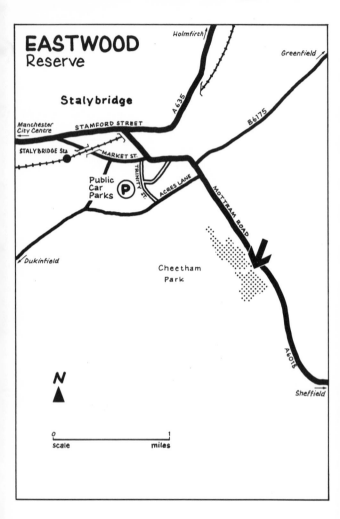

Location
Lying on the fringe of the Manchester conurbation, this educational reserve is entered from the A6018 road in Stalybridge, beside Cheetham Park, south of its junction with the A635. Public car parks are available in Trinity Street from where visitors should walk to the entrance by the Priory Tennis Club. SJ/972977.

Tenure
12 acres owned.

Warden
Richard Wakely, 12 Fir Tree Crescent, Dukinfield, SK16 5EH.

Habitat
Broadleaved woodland of sessile oak, wych elm, ash and beech in a steep-sided valley containing a stream with pools.

Birds
Grey wagtail, kingfisher and heron frequent the stream and nuthatch, great spotted woodpecker, treecreeper and tawny owl nest in the woodland. Siskin and redpoll may occur in winter and wood warbler and blackcap in summer.

Other wildlife
Toads, frogs and newts breed in the pools.

Visiting
Although primarily intended as an educational reserve with a countryside classroom for schoolchildren, members and the public are welcome to visit it on the *first* and *third Sundays* of the month or at other times by arrangement with the warden. School parties are welcome by appointment.

Facilities
IC

Town Hall Extension, Loyd Street, Manchester (tel: 061 234 3157/8).

Nearest railway station
Stalybridge (2 miles) on the main line from Manchester to Huddersfield.

Common frog

Elmley Marshes, Kent

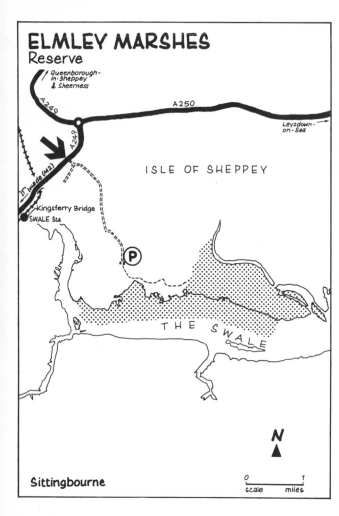

Location
Forming part of the extensive North Kent Marshes, the reserve is reached by taking the long farm track which starts from the A249 road to Sheerness one mile beyond Kingsferry bridge. TQ/926705.

Tenure
697 acres leased from Oxford University Chest and the Crown Estate Commissioners.

Status
SSSI. Grade 1.

Warden
Bob Gomes, Kingshill Farm, Elmley, Sheerness, Isle of Sheppey ME12 3RW.

Habitat
Coastal grazing marshes with freshwater fleets and shallow floods, bordered by saltmarsh on the north side of the Swale estuary.

Birds
Habitat management and wardening has made the Spitend peninsular a major refuge for thousands of wigeon, teal, mallard, shelduck and white-fronted geese in winter. The waders include black-tailed godwit, curlew, dunlin and redshank in winter when hen harrier, merlin and short-eared owl occur regularly. In the breeding season redshank, lapwing, pochard, mallard and shoveler are numerous and both avocet and black-tailed godwit may occur. Curlew sandpiper, spotted redshank and rarities such as Kentish plover use the refuge on passage.

Visiting
Open on all days *except Tuesday*, 9.00am to 9.00pm or sunset if earlier. The Spitend flooded area and saltings are overlooked by three hides which are approached by a mile walk from the reserve car park. (Elderly and disabled visitors are permitted to drive there.) Visitors are asked to keep to the main paths and below the seawall to avoid breaking the skyline and disturbing birds.

Facilities
P   **WC**   **IC**   **G** 30p

Bridge Road Car Park, Sheerness, Kent (tel: 0795 665324).

Nearest railway station
Swale (3 1/2 miles) on the branch line from Sittingbourne (main line from London, Victoria).

Wigeon

Fairburn Ings, North Yorkshire

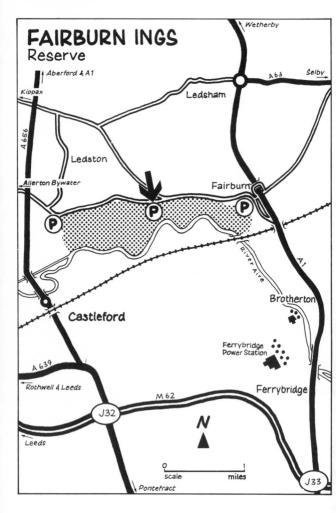

FAIRBURN INGS
Reserve

Wetherby · A63 · Selby · Aberford & A1 · Kippax · Ledsham · A656 · Ledston · Allerton Bywater · Fairburn · River Aire · A1 · Castleford · Brotherton · Ferrybridge Power Station · Ferrybridge · A639 · Rothwell & Leeds · M62 · J32 · Leeds · Pontefract · J33

N

scale   miles

Location
Lying immediately west of the A1 north of Ferrybridge, the reserve extends along the Aire valley from the village of Fairburn. SE/452278.

Tenure
680 acres leased from local authorities.

Status
SSSI. Statutory Bird Sanctuary.

Warden

Trevor Charlton, 2 Springholme, Caudle Hill, Fairburn, Knottingley WF11 9JQ.

Habitat

Large shallow lakes, marsh, scrub and flood-pools formed by mining subsidence; also deciduous woodland by the river.

Birds

Of principal importance for wintering wildfowl including mallard, teal, shoveler, pochard, tufted duck, goldeneye, goosander, coot and up to 100 whooper swans. Common, Arctic and black terns, little gull and several wader species occur on passage and both yellow and pied wagtails with swallows gather in large autumnal roosts. Lapwing, redshank, snipe, little ringed plover and both great crested and little grebes nest as do several species of ducks.

Other wildlife

Interesting marshland plants and dragonflies.

Visiting

Access at all times to three public hides overlooking the lakes which are reached via the causeway and footpath below Fairburn village. The reserve information centre with toilets, a raised boardwalk through the marsh (especially suitable for wheelchairs) and a hide beside shallow pools are situated one mile west of the village – open at weekends throughout the year from 10.00am to 5.00 pm. Otherwise good views may be obtained from the road lay-bys.

Facilities

P   WC   IC   **G** 30p

Town Hall, Wood Street, Wakefield, Yorkshire (tel: 0924 370211).

Nearest railway station

Castleford (5 miles) on the line from Wakefield to York.

Shoveler

Fore Wood, East Sussex

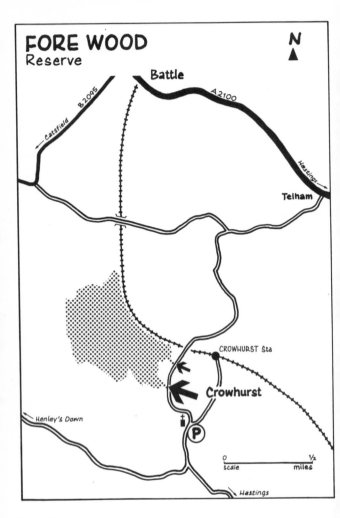

FORE WOOD
Reserve

Battle

B.2095

Catsfield

A2100

Hastings

Telham

CROWHURST Sta

Crowhurst

Henley's Down

Hastings

N

0   ½
scale miles

Location
This Wealden woodland lies on the edge of Crowhurst, two miles south-west of Telham on the A2100 Battle to Hastings road. TQ/756126.

Tenure
135 acres owned.

Status
SSSI.

Warden

Martin Allison, 2 Hale Farm Cottages, Hart Lake Road, Tudeley, Tonbridge, Kent. An assistant warden is sometimes resident.

Habitat

Undulating woodland of coppiced hornbeam and sweet chestnut with oak standards and containing glades, rides, a pond and two ravine (ghyll) streams with waterfalls.

Birds

There is a growing number of breeding birds due to habitat improvement including great, marsh and willow tits, great and lesser spotted woodpeckers, spotted flycatcher, chiffchaff, garden warbler and blackcap. Sparrowhawk, hawfinch and nightingale occur.

Other wildlife

Interesting ferns and mosses thrive in the sandstone ghylls. Bluebell, wood anemone and early purple orchid are abundant in spring. White admiral butterflies fly in the rides.

Visiting

Access at all times along a nature trail (with leaflet) which explores most of the wood. Visitors are asked to park at Crowhurst village hall opposite the church and to walk up the road to either of the reserve entrances.

Facilities

P

88 High Street, Battle, East Sussex (tel: 042 46 3721).

Nearest railway station

Crowhurst (¼ mile) on the main line from London (Charing Cross).

Hawfinch

Fowlmere, Cambridgeshire

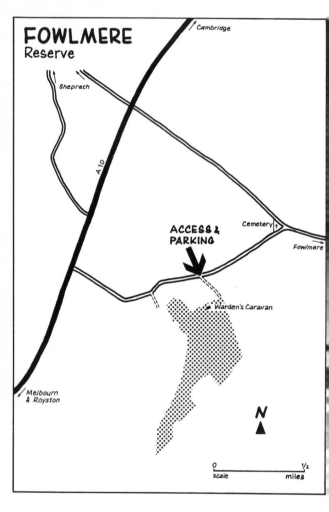

Location
Situated near Fowlmere village, the reserve is reached by turning off the A10 Cambridge to Royston road by Shepreth. TL/407461.

Tenure
85 acres owned.

Status
SSSI.

Warden
Present from April to August, c/o The Post Office, Fowlmere, Royston SG8 7SU. At other times enquiries to Reserves Division.

Habitat
An isolated fen within arable farmland comprising reeds and pools fed by spring water; also some hawthorn scrub, an alder copse and deciduous woodland.

Birds
A large colony of reed warblers nest in the reedbeds with sedge warbler, reed bunting, grasshopper warbler and water rail. Kingfishers are seen frequently and green sandpipers occur on migration. Whitethroat and turtle dove nest in the scrub which in autumn and winter is used by large flocks of fieldfare, redwing and corn bunting for roosting with pied wagtails in the reeds.

Other wildlife
Bee orchid, autumn gentian, field scabious and cowslip flower in the chalky grass areas. Frogs and toads are abundant in spring.

Visiting
Until a proper car park has been provided, cars must be parked *clear of the entrance track* on the roadside. A nature trail (with leaflet) incorporates two hides, one of which is elevated. There is a boardwalk trail for disabled visitors near the entrance.

Facilities

Wheeler Street, Cambridge (tel: 0223 322640).

Nearest railway station
Shepreth (3 miles) on the main line from London (King's Cross) to Cambridge.

Little grebe

Gayton Sands, Cheshire

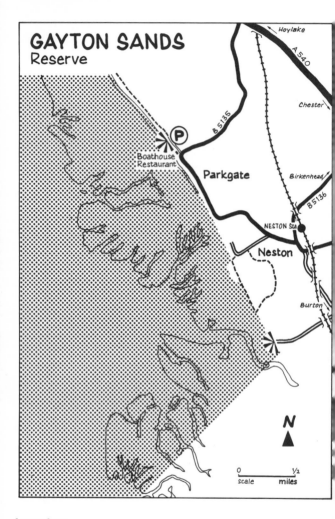

GAYTON SANDS
Reserve

Location
Occupying a large part of the east side of the Dee estuary, Gayton Sands is overlooked from Parkgate which is reached from the A540 Chester to Hoylake road via the B5135.

Tenure
5,040 acres owned.

Status
SSSI. Grade 1*.

Warden
Colin Wells, Marsh Cottage, Denhall Lane, Burton, Wirral L64 0TG.

Habitat
Extensive saltmarsh and inter-tidal sandflats, with a reedbed by the shore at Neston.

Birds
Although shelduck, oystercatcher and redshank nest on the saltmarsh, this reserve is outstanding for its large flocks of pintail, teal, mallard, wigeon and shelduck which frequent the Dee estuary in autumn and winter. Thousands of oystercatcher, grey plover, knot, dunlin, curlew, redshank and bar-tailed godwit assemble on the foreshore where peregrine, merlin and hen harrier often hunt. Twite and brambling often occur.

Visiting
Good birdwatching, especially at high tides (times are available from the warden), can be obtained from the Old Baths car park and the adjacent public footpath, located near the Boathouse Restaurant (SJ/274789). Visitors are advised *not* to venture onto the saltmarsh because of very dangerous tides.

Facilities
P

Town Hall, Northgate Street, Chester, Cheshire (tel: 0244 40144).

Nearest railway station
Neston (1 mile) on the line from Wrexham Central to Liverpool.

Shelduck

Geltsdale, Cumbria

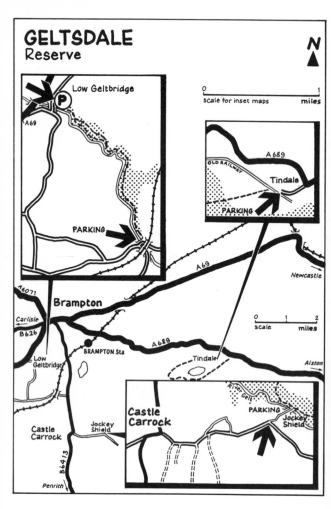

Location

Lying within the northern Pennines, the fells of the King's Forest of Geltsdale rise south of the A69 road from Carlisle to Newcastle and may be viewed from the A689 east of Brampton. The reserve also includes several woods in the nearby valleys of the Rivers Gelt and Irthing.

Tenure

12,000 acres of moorland is a reserve by agreement with the owners, while 300 acres of woodland are managed by agreement with several owners.

Status
The moorland is SSSI, Grade 1. Gelt Woods are SSSI.

Warden
John Miles, Jockey Shield, Castle Carrock, near Carlisle, Cumbria.

Habitat
Mainly heather moorland rising to the 2,000 feet summit of Coldfell, with a tarn and mixed deciduous woodland on steep valley sides.

Birds
Red grouse, golden plover, curlew, ring ouzel and lapwing nest on the fells and the pastures below them. Large populations of pied flycatcher, redstart, wood warbler and several sparrowhawks breed in the woodland, while the streams hold dipper, grey wagtail, goosander and common sandpiper. Whooper swans and goldeneye visit Tindale Tarn in winter.

Other wildlife
Some meadows contain globe flower, common wintergreen and bird's-nest orchid. Red squirrels and roe deer inhabit the riverside woods.

Visiting
While access is not permitted to the Geltsdale moorland, it may be viewed from bridleways starting either at Jockey Shield (NY/561557) east of Castle Carrock or along the old railway line from Tindale off the A689 (NY/616593). A waymarked path runs through the *Lower Gelt Woods*, joining the reserve at Gelt Bridge (NY/520592), with car park, off the A69 from Carlisle 1½ miles south of Brampton, or by the railway viaduct (NY/533573) west of the B6413 road to Castle Carrock three miles south of Brampton — the latter being suitable for wheelchairs.

Facilities
P

Moot Hall, Brampton, Cumbria (tel: 069 77 3433).

Nearest railway station
Brampton on the line from Carlisle to Newcastle.

Havergate Island, Suffolk

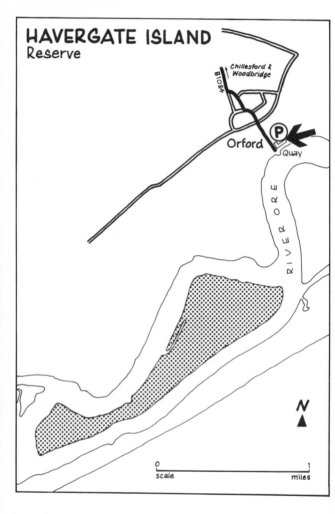

HAVERGATE ISLAND
Reserve

Chillesford &
Woodbridge

B1084

Orford

P

Quay

RIVER ORE

N

0 scale 1 miles

Location
Lying within the River Ore on the Suffolk coast, the island is reached by boat from Orford quay. TM/425496.

Tenure
267 acres owned.

Status
SSSI. Grade 1. Also part of a National Nature Reserve.

Warden
John Partridge, 30 Mundays Lane, Orford, Woodbridge IP12 2LX.

Habitat
A low embanked island in the River Ore containing shallow, brackish water lagoons with islands and surrounded by saltmarsh and shingle beaches.

Birds
Britain's largest nesting colony of avocets was established here in 1947 and now numbers some 120 pairs. Sandwich and common terns, oystercatcher, ringed plover, redshank and shelduck also breed and several wader species occur on passage. Many avocets remain over winter when teal, wigeon, pintail, shoveler, mallard and occasionally Bewick's swan and hen harrier are present.

Other wildlife
Sea purslane and sea lavender flower on the saltings and sea pea and English stonecrop on the shingle beach. Roesel's bush cricket is a speciality in late summer.

Visiting
Boat trips are run to the island between April and August on *Saturdays, Sundays, Mondays* and *Thursdays,* leaving Orford quay at 10.00am and 11.30am. Permits must be obtained by written application *only* from the warden (charge: members £1.50, non-members £3.50 – enclosed with application). Visiting during September-March is on alternate Thursdays and Saturdays: the dates are obtainable from the warden. There are several hides with an information centre, basic toilets and a picnic area on the island.

Facilities
IC   **G** 30p

The Cinema, High Street, Aldeburgh, Suffolk (tel: 072 885 3637).

Nearest railway station
Wickham Market (8 miles) on the line from Ipswich (main line from London, Liverpool Street) to Lowestoft.

Hornsea Mere, Humberside

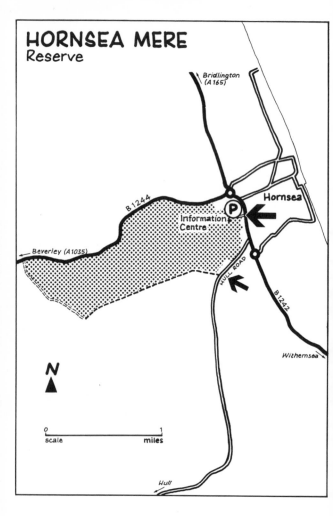

HORNSEA MERE
Reserve

Bridlington
(A 165)

B 1244

Hornsea

Information
Centre

Beverley (A1035)

HULL ROAD

B 1242

Withernsea

N

0   1
scale   miles

Hull

Location
The reserve information centre is situated at the east end of the mere and is reached from the centre of Hornsea by taking the side roads signposted to The Mere. TA/202474.

Tenure
580 acres leased from the Wassand Estate.

Status
SSSI. Grade 1. Also a Statutory Bird Sanctuary.

Warden
Ivan Proctor, The Bungalow, The Mere, Hornsea HU18 1AX.

Habitat
A large natural, freshwater lake, reed-fringed and bordered by mixed woodland and farmland close to the sea.

Birds
Hundreds of reed warblers nest here as well as sedge warbler, reed bunting, coot and great crested grebe. Cormorants roost in the lakeside trees. Little gulls and black terns are often numerous on summer passage and wheatear, whinchat and various warblers pass during the spring. Winter brings large concentrations of goldeneye, mallard, coot, wigeon, teal, pochard and tufted duck to the mere.

Visiting
Cars may be parked by the information centre on Kirkholme Point (by kind permission of the Hornsea Mere Marine Company) where a cafeteria and boating are also available. A public footpath along the south side of the mere, starting in Hull Road, affords good birdwatching. No other access is permitted to the reserve.

Facilities
P   **WC**   **IC**   **G** 30p

Floral Hall, Esplanade, Hornsea, Humberside (tel: 040 12 2919).

Nearest railway station
Beverley (12 miles) on the line from Hull to Scarborough.

Reed warbler

Langstone Harbour, Hampshire

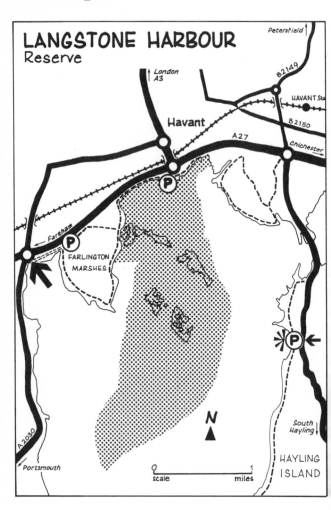

LANGSTONE HARBOUR Reserve

Petersfield
London A3
B2149
HAVANT Sta
Havant
B2150
A27
Chichester
Fareham
FARLINGTON MARSHES
A2030
Portsmouth

N

scale 0 — 1 miles

South Hayling
HAYLING ISLAND

Location
Occupying a central portion of Langstone Harbour, the reserve's low islands and mudflats may be viewed from the coastal footpath along the northern shore, also from the seawall of Farlington Marshes (a reserve of the Hampshire and Isle of Wight Naturalists' Trust).

Tenure
1,370 acres owned.

Status
SSSI. Grade 1*.

Warden
Present from April to August and occasionally in other months:
c/o Reserves Division (see page 7).

Habitat
Mudflats, creeks and saltmarsh islands.

Birds
The islands are the site of one of Britain's largest little tern colonies
which numbered over 100 pairs in 1986. Common tern, ringed
plover and redshank also breed there. The entire harbour is
outstanding for wintering wildfowl including over 7,000 brent
geese as well as teal, wigeon, shelduck, dunlin, oystercatcher,
curlew and black-tailed godwit. Black-necked grebe, red-breasted
merganser and greenshank occur regularly outside the breeding
season.

Visiting
There is no official reserve entrance but access to the coastal
footpath, and good viewpoints, may be gained from the roundabout junction of the A2030 and A27 Chichester to Fareham road
(SU/675043): also by the roundabout at the junction of the A3 and
A27 where there is a car park (SU/697056). Another viewpoint is
from the car park off the Hayling Island road by the Esso Garage
(SU/718029). Boat-users are not permitted to land on any of the
reserve islands except Long Island.

The Hard, Portsmouth, Hampshire (tel: 0705 826722/3).

Nearest railway station
Havant on the main line from London (Waterloo).

Common tern

Leighton Moss, Lancashire

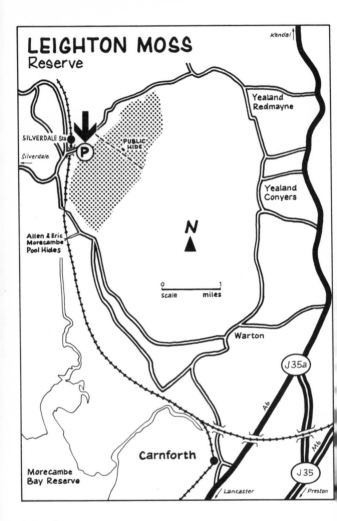

LEIGHTON MOSS Reserve

Kendal

Yealand Redmayne

SILVERDALE Sta

Silverdale

PUBLIC HIDE

Allen & Eric Morecambe Pool Hides

Yealand Conyers

N

0 scale 1 miles

Warton

J35a

A6

Carnforth

Morecambe Bay Reserve

Lancaster

J35

Preston

M6

Location
Lying in a limestone valley close to the shore of Morecambe Bay, the reserve is entered close to Silverdale station and is reached from the A6(T) through Carnforth, Yealand Conyers or Yealand Redmayne. SD/478751.

Tenure
321 acres owned.

Status
SSSI. Grade 1.

Warden

John Wilson, Myers Farm, Silverdale, Carnforth LA5 0SW (tel: 0524 701601).

Habitat

A large reedswamp with meres and willow and alder scrub in a valley, with woodland on its limestone slopes.

Birds

Britain's largest concentration of up to a dozen pairs of bitterns breed here, together with bearded tit, reed, sedge and grass-hopper warblers, teal, shoveler, tufted duck and occasionally garganey. Black tern, osprey, and marsh harrier regularly pass through in spring and greenshank and various sandpipers in autumn. Wintering wildfowl include large flocks of mallard, teal, wigeon, pintail and shoveler. Thousands of starlings, swallows and wagtails roost seasonally in the reeds, often attracting hunting sparrowhawks.

Other wildlife

Otters are resident and are frequently seen from the hides, as are roe and red deer.

Visiting

Open on all days *except Tuesday*, 9.00am to 9.00pm or sunset when earlier. £2.00 charge for non-members. Five hides over-looking various meres are linked by paths through the reeds. One is on the public causeway and is open, free of charge, at all times. The reserve Centre contains interpretative displays, an exhibition, shop and toilets.

Facilities

P   WC   IC   S   &   G 50p

i

Marine Road Central, Morecambe, Lancashire (tel: 0524 414110).

Details of local accommodation are displayed on the Centre's noticeboard. See advertisement page 70.

Nearest railway station

Silverdale (¼ mile) on the line from Lancaster (main line from London, Euston) to Barrow-in-Furness.

The Lodge, Bedfordshire

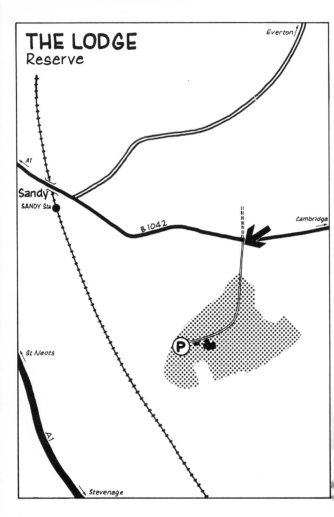

Location
The headquarters of the RSPB and its surrounding reserve is entered from the B1042 road to Cambridge, a mile east of Sandy which is on the A1. TL/192486.

Tenure
104 acres owned.

Status
Partly SSSI.

Warden
Gary Pilkington, The Lodge, Sandy SG19 2DL (tel: 0767 80551).

Habitat
Mature woodland, fir plantations, birch and bracken slopes on a ridge of Lower Greensand with a remnant of heath and an artificial lake. Formal gardens adjoin the Victorian mansion.

Birds
Breeding birds include kestrel, all three woodpeckers, nuthatch, treecreeper, blackcap, garden warbler, moorhen and tree pipit. Kingfisher, heron, sparrowhawk and crossbill are occasionally seen. Finches including siskin and redpoll occur in winter.

Other wildlife
Muntjac deer are often seen. Several species of dragonflies frequent the lake in summer. There is an important breeding colony of natterjack toads.

Visiting
The reserve and formal gardens are open on all days from 9.00am to 9.00pm or sunset when earlier. The shop and reception with its exhibition is open all year 9.00am to 5.00pm weekdays; 10.00am to 5.00pm weekends (except for Christmas to Easter which is 12.00pm to 4.30pm). The house and other premises, being administrative offices, are *not* open to members or the public. There are three nature trails of various lengths (with leaflet) around the reserve and a hide overlooks the lake.

Facilities
P   WC   IC   S   &   G 40p

10 St Paul's Square, Bedford (tel: 0234 215226).

Nearest railway station
Sandy (1½ miles) on the main line from London (Kings Cross).

Woodcock

73

Lodmoor, Dorset

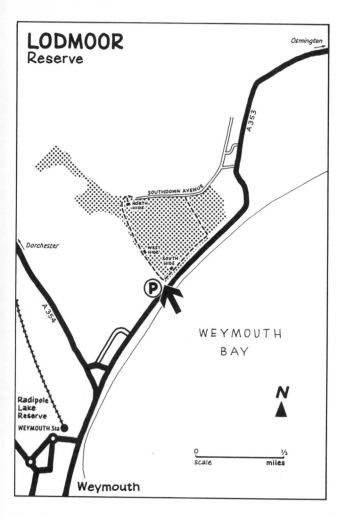

LODMOOR
Reserve

Osmington

A 353

SOUTHDOWN AVENUE

Dorchester

NORTH HIDE

WEST HIDE
SOUTH HIDE

P

A 354

WEYMOUTH BAY

N

Radipole Lake Reserve

WEYMOUTH Sta

0 — scale — ½ miles

Weymouth

Location
Situated near the beach on the east side of Weymouth, the reserve is entered from the car park for Lodmoor Country Park on the A353 road to Wareham by the Sea Life Centre. SY/687807.

Tenure
150 acres leased from Weymouth Borough Council.

Status
SSSI.

Warden
Doug Ireland, c/o Radipole Lake Reserve, (see page 95).

Habitat
A marsh with shallow pools, reeds and scrub as well as remnant saltmarsh inside the seawall.

Birds
The reedbeds and scrub contain reed, sedge and grasshopper warblers, bearded tit, reed bunting and Cetti's warbler, while mallard, redshank and yellow wagtail breed on the marsh. Thousands of yellow wagtails congregate on migration and a variety of waders such as sanderling use the pools to feed and rest. Wintering wildfowl include mallard, teal, shoveler, wigeon, shelduck and brent geese.

Visiting
Access at all times from the public car park to a perimeter path which links three hides overlooking the marsh and reedbeds. See under Radipole Lake for the Weymouth car parking concession (page 95).

Facilities
P   WC

Pavilion Theatre Complex, The Esplanade, Weymouth, Dorset (tel: 0305 772444).

See advertisements page 79.

Nearest railway station
Weymouth (1½ miles) on the main line from London (Waterloo).

Wigeon

Minsmere, Suffolk

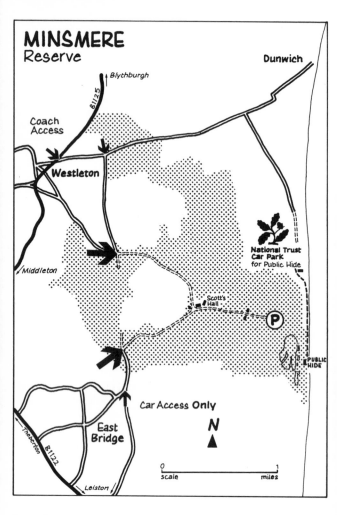

MINSMERE Reserve

Dunwich

↑ Blythburgh

B1125

Coach Access

Westleton

Middleton

National Trust Car Park for Public Hide

Scott's Hall

P

PUBLIC HIDE

Car Access Only

N ▲

Theberton

B1122

East Bridge

Leiston

0 — scale — 1 miles

Location
Lying on the low Suffolk coast, this premier RSPB reserve is reached either from Westleton or through East Bridge (*no coaches this way*) from the B1122 road from Leiston to Yoxford. It is clearly signposted in the vicinity. TM/452680.

Tenure
1,470 acres owned.

Status
SSSI. Grade 1*. Council of Europe Diploma.

Warden

Jeremy Sorensen, Minsmere Reserve, Westleton, Saxmundham IP17 2BY (tel: 072 873 281).

Habitat

The famous Scrape – an area of shallow brackish water, mud and islands inside the shingle beach – as well as extensive reedbeds with meres and both heathland and deciduous woodland.

Birds

A large variety of breeding birds include common tern and Britain's second largest avocet colony on the Scrape; little tern on the beach; bittern, marsh harrier, bearded tit and water rail in the reeds; nightjar and stonechat on the heath and nightingale and redstart in the woods. Many different waders such as spotted redshank, black-tailed godwit, little stint and several rarities use the Scrape on migration. Bewick's swan, wigeon, gadwall and teal occur in winter.

Other wildlife

Coypus and otters frequent the marshes while adders and silver-studded blue butterflies are encountered on the heath.

Visiting

Open on all days *except Tuesday*, 9.00am to 9.00pm or sunset when earlier. However, *only members may visit on Sundays and over Bank Holiday weekends.* £2.00 charge for non-members. Car drivers are asked to take special care on the narrow lanes within and approaching the reserve. The public hide on the beach overlooking the Scrape, is always open (free of charge) and is reached on foot from Dunwich Cliffs National Trust car park. (TM/475680).

Facilities

P   **WC**   **IC**   **S**   ♿   **G** 50p

Town Hall, High Street, Southwold, Suffolk (tel: 0502 722366).

See advertisements page 78.

Nearest railway station

Saxmundham (6 miles) on the line from Ipswich (main line from London, Liverpool Street) to Lowestoft.

79

Morecambe Bay, Lancashire

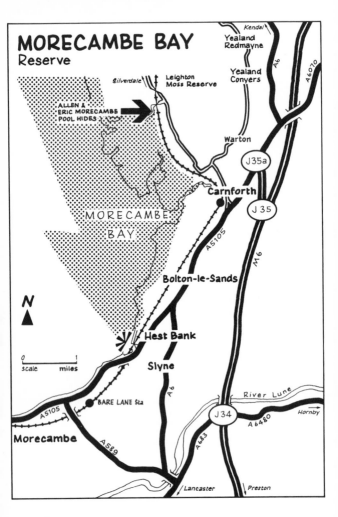

Location

The eastern side of this vast estuary may be viewed from several vantage points, notably the car park across the level-crossing at Hest Bank off the A5105 Morecambe to Carnforth road. (SD/468666). A small car park off the Carnforth to Silverdale road near Leighton Moss reserve (see page 68) provides access to hides overlooking a lagoon on the Carnforth saltings (SD/476737).

Tenure

3,750 acres owned, together with a further 2,400 acres of freehold rights.

Status
SSSI. Grade 1*.

Warden
John Wilson, c/o Leighton Moss Reserve (see page 68).

Birds
Of outstanding importance for its very large flocks of waders such as knot, dunlin, oystercatcher, curlew, bar-tailed godwit and redshank which congregate, according to the tides, during most of the year except mid-summer. Sanderling occur on May migration. Peregrines frequently hunt the waders in winter when shelduck, pintail, wigeon, red-breasted merganser and greylag are present. Oystercatcher, redshank and wheatear nest on the saltings.

Other wildlife
Bloody cranesbill, rock-rose and rock samphire flower on the limestone cliffs behind the marsh at Silverdale.

Visiting
Access to Hest Bank and the Carnforth Marsh pool hides at all times. Tide times are available from Leighton Moss reserve. Visitors are warned to beware of dangerous channels and quicksands on the foreshore.

Facilities
P (Hest Bank)

Marine Road Central, Morecambe, Lancashire (tel: 0524 414110).

See advertisement page 70.

Nearest railway station
Silverdale (1 mile to Carnforth Marsh) and Bare Lane (2 miles to Hest Bank) on the line from Lancaster (main line from London, Euston) to Barrow-in-Furness.

Oystercatcher

Nagshead, Gloucestershire

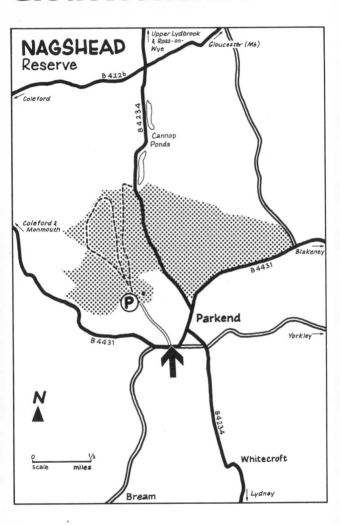

NAGSHEAD Reserve

Upper Lydbrook & Ross-on-Wye

Gloucester (M6)

B 422b

Coleford

B 4234

Cannop Ponds

Coleford & Monmouth

Blakeney

B 4431

P

Parkend

Yorkley

B 4431

N

B 4234

0   ½
scale   miles

Whitecroft

Lydney

Bream

Location
Forming part of the ancient Forest of Dean, this reserve is situated immediately west of Parkend village and is entered up a forest track off the B4431 road to Coleford. SO/612078.

Tenure
761 acres managed by agreement with the Forestry Commission.

Status
SSSI. Grade 1.

Warden

Ian Bullock, 6 Stompers Row, Parkend, Lydney GL15 4JL.

Habitat

Mature oakwood with beech, birch, rowan and holly and containing a rocky stream with a pool and clumps of alder and firs.

Birds

A large population of pied flycatchers nest mainly in boxes, as do some of the redstarts, great and blue tits and nuthatches. Other breeding species include wood warbler, chiffchaff, tree pipit, blackcap, garden warbler, treecreeper and the three species of woodpeckers. Sparrowhawk, crossbill and hawfinch are seen regularly.

Other wildlife

Bluebells and foxgloves are abundant. Silver-washed and pearl-bordered fritillaries and white admiral butterflies occur as do dormice and fallow deer.

Visiting

Access at all times from the reserve car park and picnic area. Visitors are asked to keep to the waymarked paths of ½ mile and 2 miles in length, off which there are two hides overlooking glades and a pool.

Facilities

P   **WC**   **IC**   **G** 30p

Cinderford Library, Bell View Road, Cinderford, Gloucestershire (tel: Dean 0594 22581).

Nearest railway station

Lydney (6 miles) on the line from Gloucester to Cardiff Central.

Pied flycatcher

Nene Washes, Cambridgeshire

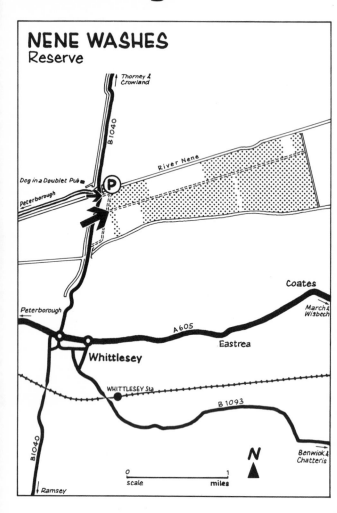

Location
This Fenland reserve is situated five miles east of Peterborough and is entered off the B1040 road from Whittlesey to Thorney. TL/277992.

Tenure
582 acres owned.

Status
SSSI. Grade 1.

Warden
Geoff Welch, 21a East Delph, Whittlesey, near Peterborough
PE7 1RH.

Habitat
A three-mile stretch of wet meadows with a bunded area of
marshland between two embanked rivers.

Birds
Redshank, snipe, sedge warbler, yellow wagtail, shoveler, mallard,
gadwall and shelduck nest regularly with garganey in some years.
Black-tailed godwit, marsh harrier and hobby occur in summer
while several waders such as greenshank pause on migration.
When flooding occurs in winter large flocks of Bewick's swan,
wigeon, teal, shoveler and pintail visit the reserve.

Visiting
Until proper facilities have been installed, members and the public
are welcome to visit the reserve *by written application to the
warden.*

Facilities
P

Town Hall, Bridge Street, Peterborough, Cambridgeshire (tel:
0733 63141).

Nearest railway station
Whittlesey (2 miles) on the line from Peterborough (main line
from London, King's Cross) to Ely.

Black-tailed godwit

Northward Hill, Kent

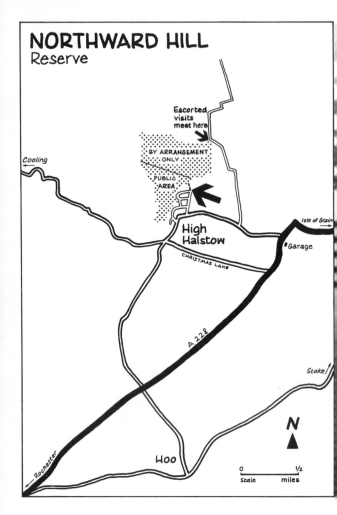

NORTHWARD HILL
Reserve

Escorted visits meet here

BY ARRANGEMENT ONLY

PUBLIC AREA

Cooling

Isle of Grain

High Halstow

Garage

CHRISTMAS LANE

A 228

Stoke

Rochester

Hoo

N

0   ½
scale   miles

Location
Overlooking the Thames marshes north of Rochester, the reserve lies on rising ground at the edge of High Halstow which is reached via the A228 road to the Isle of Grain. It is entered across a field from Northwood Avenue in High Halstow. TQ/784759.

Tenure
134 acres owned.

Status
SSSI. Grade 2. Also a National Nature Reserve.

Warden

Alan Parker, Swigshole Cottage, High Halstow, Rochester ME3 8SR.

Habitat

Deciduous woodland of oak, ash and maple with elm scrub and dense thickets of hawthorn.

Birds

The location of Britain's largest heronry of some 220 pairs which feed on the marshes below. Many nightingale and turtle dove breed as well as whitethroat, lesser whitethroat, garden warbler, blackcap and both great and lesser spotted woodpeckers. Merlin and sparrowhawk frequently hunt the thrush roosts in winter.

Other wildlife

A thriving colony of white-letter hairstreak butterflies occupies the elm scrub. Essex skipper and speckled wood also occur.

Visiting

The paths in the public part of the reserve are accessible at all times. Escorted access to the sanctuary area, including the heronry viewpoint, may be arranged by written application to the warden (charge £1 to non-members), the herons being present from February to July. Please note that coaches are not advisable owing to the difficulties of parking in High Halstow.

Eastgate Cottage, High Street, Rochester, Kent (tel: Medway 0634 43666).

Nearest railway station

Rochester (6 miles) on the main line from London (Victoria).

Heron

North Warren, Suffolk

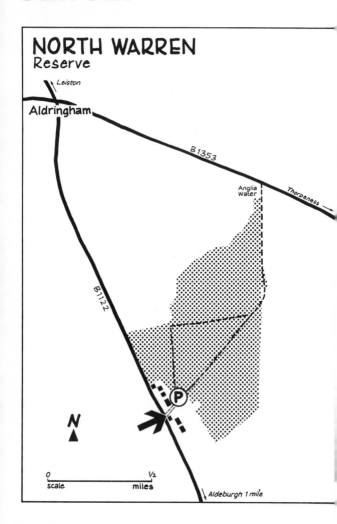

Location
Part of the Sandlings heathland of the Suffolk coast, this reserve lies on the east side of the B1122 road to Leiston a mile north of Aldeburgh. The reserve car park is entered, as signposted, between the neighbouring houses. TM/455587.

Tenure
237 acres owned.

Status
SSSI.

Warden

None present. Enquiries to Minsmere Reserve (see page 76).

Habitat

A grass heath with areas of gorse and birch scrub on sandy soil, together with a mature fen with reeds, meadowsweet and sallow.

Birds

Yellowhammer, skylark, linnet, whitethroat and nightingale nest on the scrubby heath where wheatears occur on migration. Reed, sedge and grasshopper warblers and reed bunting frequent the fen and both kingfisher and bearded tit are seen occasionally.

Other wildlife

Viper's bugloss, mullein and tree lupin flower on the heath.

Visiting

Access at all times to a nature trail (with leaflet) which explores the reserve.

Facilities

P

The Cinema, High Street, Aldeburgh, Suffolk (tel: 072 885 3637).

See advertisements page 78.

Nearest railway station

Saxmundham (6 miles) on the line from Ipswich (main line from London, Liverpool Street) to Lowestoft.

Nightingale

Old Hall Marshes, Essex

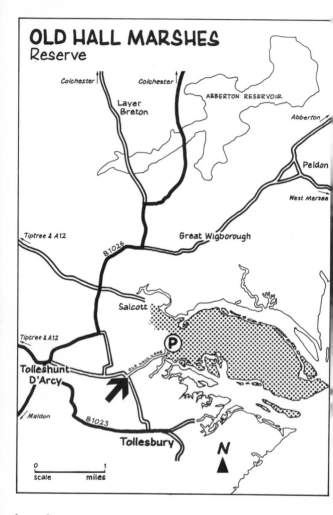

OLD HALL MARSHES
Reserve

Colchester — Layer Breton

Colchester — ABBERTON RESERVOIR

Abberton

Peldon

West Mersea

Tiptree & A12

B1026

Great Wigborough

Salcott

Tiptree & A12

Tolleshunt D'Arcy

Maldon

B1023

OLD HALL LANE

P

Tollesbury

N

0   1
scale   miles

Location
This remote peninsular at the mouth of the Blackwater estuary is entered at its western end from the minor road between Tollesbury and Tolleshunt D'Arcy. TL/950117.

Tenure
1,118 acres owned and 442 acres leased from the Nature Conservancy Council.

Status
SSSI. Grade 1*.

Warden
Peter Gotham, 1 Old Hall Lane, Tollesbury, near Maldon, Essex.

Habitat
Extensive grazing marshes with freshwater fleets and reedbeds, saltings and two small offshore islands.

Birds
Up to 4,000 brent geese feed on the improved pasture each winter when thousands of wigeon, teal, shelduck, grey plover, curlew, redshank and dunlin frequent the marshes. Divers and goldeneye are seen on the adjacent channels and short-eared owl, hen harrier, barn owl and merlin regularly hunt the reserve. Breeding species include redshank, pochard, shoveler, bearded tit, water rail and common tern. Waders such as avocet visit on migration.

Visiting
Several public footpaths provide good views of the reserve and its birds. Visitors are asked to walk below the seawall to avoid disturbing birds on the mudflats. There is limited car parking at the entrance to the reserve but cars must *not* be parked on the private approach road. Facilities including hides are planned for the future.

Facilities
P

2 High Street, Maldon, Essex (tel: 0621 56503).

Nearest railway station
Kelvedon (9 miles) on the main line from London (Liverpool Street).

Curlew

Ouse Washes, Cambridgeshire

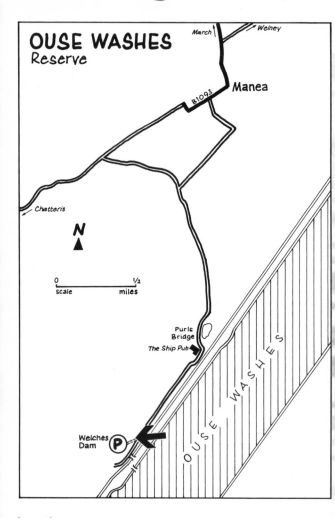

Location
Part of a 19-mile stretch of flood washland, the RSPB reserve is entered at Welches Dam which is signposted from Manea village. Approach via the B1093 or B1098 roads from the A141 road from Chatteris to March. TL/471861. (Nb: the area hatched is not entirely owned by the RSPB.)

Tenure
1,747 acres owned.

Status
SSSI. Grade 1*.

Warden
Cliff Carson, Limosa, Welches Dam, Manea, March PE15 0ND.

Habitat
Extensive wet meadowland or 'washes', dissected by numerous ditches and contained by two parallel rivers that were excavated in the 17th century. Several osier beds grow by the River Delph.

Birds
The largest concentration of black-tailed godwits in Britain (up to 40 pairs) breed on this and the adjacent Wildfowl Trust and Cambridgeshire and Isle of Ely Naturalists' Trust reserves, their success depending on the state of flooding in the spring. Ruffs 'lek' annually and may nest, other species being shoveler, teal, garganey, yellow wagtail, redshank and snipe. In winter, when the washes are flooded, this becomes the most important site inland in Britain for wildfowl including some 5,000 Bewick's swans and large numbers of wigeon, teal, pintail and mallard as well as shoveler, whooper swan, hen harrier and short-eared owl.

Visiting
Access at all times from the reserve car park, with Information Centre and toilets, to a series of hides sited along the flood bank and overlooking the washes. Visitors are requested to walk *below* the bank to avoid disturbing the birds. *Sundays* are preferable during September-January which is the wildfowling season on several adjacent non-reserve washes.

Facilities
P   WC   IC   G 30p

Public Library, Palace Green, Ely, Cambridgeshire (tel: 0353 2062).

Nearest railway station
Manea (4 miles) on the line from Ely (main line from London, Liverpool Street) to Peterborough.

Bewick's swan

Radipole Lake, Dorset

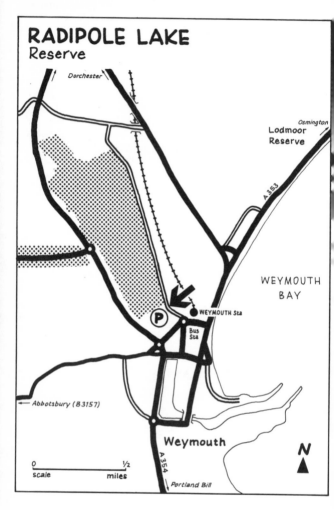

RADIPOLE LAKE
Reserve

Dorchester

Osmington

Lodmoor
Reserve

A 353

WEYMOUTH
BAY

P

WEYMOUTH Sta

Bus
Sta

Abbotsbury (B3157)

Weymouth

A 354

Portland Bill

0   ½
scale   miles

N

Location
Situated within the town of Weymouth, the reserve information
centre and entrance are located beside the Swannery public car
park which is signposted from the main street along the seafront.
SY/677796.

Tenure
192 acres leased from Weymouth Borough Council.

Status
SSSI. Also Statutory Bird Sanctuary.

Warden

Doug Ireland, 52 Goldcroft Avenue, Weymouth, Dorset DT4 0ES.

Habitat

Large reedbeds and lakes with rough pasture, scrub and some artificial shallow lagoons.

Birds

Reed, sedge and grasshopper warblers, bearded tit, great crested grebe, mute swan, kingfisher and many pairs of Cetti's warbler breed here, while heron, cormorant, shelduck and sparrowhawk visit regularly. Up to 100 mute swans congregate to moult, while considerable numbers of yellow wagtails, sedge warblers and swallows roost in the reeds during migration. Mediterranean and other uncommon species of gulls occur. Shoveler, teal and pochard are among the wintering duck.

Other wildlife

Interesting dragonflies include the emperor.

Visiting

Access to the reserve at all times. The Centre (with its panoramic window overlooking the lake) is open daily April-September, weekends only October-March. Public toilets are available in the adjacent car park (for which there is a charge). A ticket purchased first in the Swannery car park allows parking without charge in that for Lodmoor (p 74). Firm paths lead to three hides, one of which is for members only. The facilities have all been designed with the needs of handicapped visitors particularly in mind including 'listening posts' and a tap-rail on the trail.

Facilities

P   **WC**   **IC**   ♿   **G** 50p

Pavilion Theatre Complex, The Esplanade, Weymouth, Dorset (tel: 0305 772444).

See advertisements page 79.

Nearest railway station

Weymouth (adjacent) on main line from London (Waterloo).

Rye House Marsh, Hertfordshire

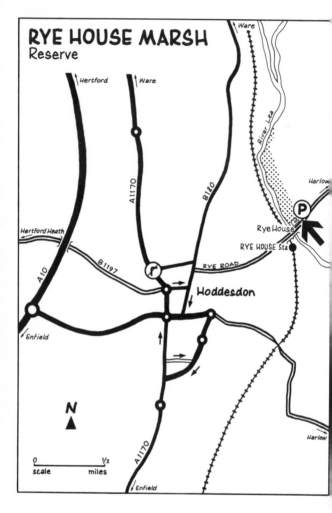

Location
Lying within the Lee Valley Regional Park, this reserve is approached from the A10 in Hoddesdon by taking Rye Road and entering the car park just past Rye House railway station. TL/387099.

Tenure
13 acres leased from the Lee Valley Regional Park Authority.

Warden
Kevin Roberts, Toad Cottage, 4 Cecil Road, Rye Park, Hoddesdon EN11 0JA.

Habitat

A riverside marsh containing a variety of habitats including shallow pools and mud, fen, stands of reed sweet-grass, willow and alder scrub and wet meadow.

Birds

Mallard, tufted duck, coot, reed, sedge and grasshopper warblers and spotted flycatcher nest regularly here and Cetti's warblers have occurred. Green and common sandpipers, spotted redshank and yellow wagtail occur on migration, while many snipe, teal, corn bunting and meadow pipit are present in winter when kingfisher, water rail, jack snipe, siskin and occasionally bearded tit may be seen.

Other wildlife

Pink water speedwell, fen bedstraw and ragged robin are among the plants.

Visiting

Although this is primarily an educational reserve for schoolchildren, members and the public are welcome to visit it at weekends (9.00am to 9.00pm or sunset when earlier) or at other times by written application to the warden. There is ample car parking and an Information Centre, with public toilets nearby. One hide (accessible to wheelchairs) lies along a short, concrete path; the others are more distant and accessible only by permit, being open for more limited hours. Educational staff are available to receive schoolchildren or groups in further education, by appointment, for field studies.

Common terns nest on an adjacent lagoon and may be watched from a hide by permission of the Thames Water Authority – enquire at the reserve.

Facilities

P   **WC**   **IC**   ♿

Vale House, 43 Cowbridge, Hertford (tel: 0279 55261).

Nearest railway station

Rye House (¼ mile) on the main line from London (Liverpool Street).

St Bees Head, Cumbria

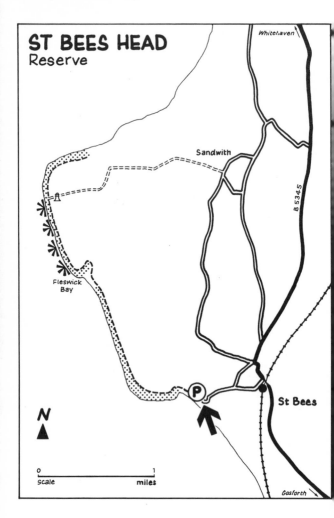

ST BEES HEAD
Reserve

Whitehaven

Sandwith

B 5345

Fleswick
Bay

St Bees

N

Gosforth

scale   miles
0   1

Location
This cliff headland lies south of Whitehaven and west of the B5345 road to St Bees.

Tenure
1¼ miles of cliffs, in two parts, owned.

Status
SSSI.

Warden

Present from April to August, c/o St Bees Head Lighthouse, Sandwith, Whitehaven, Cumbria.

Habitat

Sandstone cliffs, up to 300ft high, with many ledges and grassy tops with gorse patches.

Birds

One of the largest cliff seabird colonies on the west coast of England containing razorbill, guillemot, kittiwake, herring gull, fulmar, a small number of puffins and the only black guillemots breeding in England. Rock pipit, raven, peregrine, stonechat, whitethroat, shag and cormorant also frequent the cliffs. Gannet, skuas, terns, shearwaters and eider may be seen offshore at various times.

Other wildlife

Rock samphire, bloody cranesbill and heath spotted orchid flower on the cliff-top.

Visiting

A public footpath from the public car park (NX/962118), on St Bees beach goes north along the cliffs to four safe observation points. Only cars with disabled visitors may use the private road to the lighthouse from Sandwith — otherwise *no access*. Visitors should not attempt to reach the beach between the north and south headlands other than at Fleswick Bay.

Facilities

P   **WC**

Market Place, Whitehaven, Cumbria (tel: 0946 5678).

See advertisement page 100.

Nearest railway station

St Bees (½ mile) on the line from Carlisle to Barrow-in-Furness.

Puffin

Sandwell Valley, Birmingham

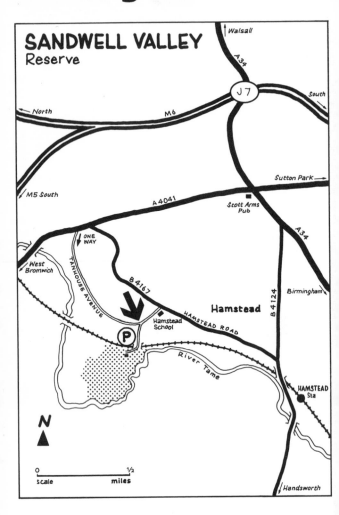

Location
Forming part of the Sandwell Valley Country Park only four miles from the centre of Birmingham, the reserve is entered off Tanhouse Avenue which is reached via Hamstead Road in Great Barr. SP/036931.

Tenure
25 acres leased from Sandwell Valley Borough Council.

Warden
Andy Warren, RSPB Nature Centre, 20 Tanhouse Avenue, Great Barr B43 5AG (tel: 021 358 3013).

Habitat
Part of a lake with an island, bordered by a marsh with willows, reed sweet-grass and shallow pools.

Birds
Breeding birds include mallard, tufted duck, coot, moorhen, little ringed plover, lapwing, snipe, reed, sedge and willow warblers, whitethroat and willow tit. Common tern and great crested grebe occur in the summer. Curlew, dunlin, green and common sandpipers and greenshank visit on migration. Wigeon and pochard frequent the lake in winter, with teal in the marsh where snipe, jack snipe and water rail may be seen daily.

Other wildlife
Many species of butterflies are seen each year. Chicory and coltsfoot flower on the higher ground.

Visiting
Access at all times to the car park from where a firm path leads downhill to two hides by the lake and marsh. The Information Centre, with toilets, provides a panoramic view of the reserve. School parties from primary to sixth-form level are welcome by appointment.

Facilities
P   IC   WC   ♿

The Piazza National Exhibition Centre, Birmingham (tel: 021 780 4141).

Nearest railway station
Hamstead (1 mile) on the line from central Birmingham.

Tufted duck

Snettisham, Norfolk

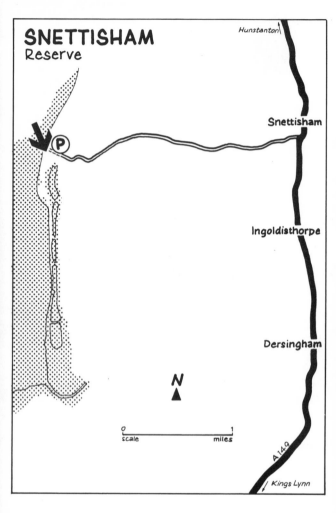

Location
Occupying part of the east shore of the Wash estuary, the beach and reserve are reached from Snettisham village on the A149 road from King's Lynn to Hunstanton. TF/648335.

Tenure
107 acres owned and 3,150 acres leased from three owners.

Status
SSSI. Grade 1*.

Warden

18 Cockle Road, Snettisham, near King's Lynn, Norfolk PE31 6HD.

Habitat

A shingle beach containing flooded pits borders a vast expanse of tidal sand and mudflats with saltmarsh.

Birds

In winter up to 70,000 waders roost off the beach and on the artificial islands of the sanctuary pit during high tides. These include knot, grey plover, bar-tailed godwit, oystercatcher, dunlin, redshank, curlew, turnstone and ringed plover. Thousands of pink-footed and brent geese with shelduck, mallard, wigeon and teal use the foreshore for feeding and roosting. Diving ducks such as red-breasted merganser and tufted duck also frequent the pits which in summer have a nesting colony of common terns. Large numbers of sanderling and several passerines such as wheatear pause on migration.

Other wildlife

The shingle beach flora includes yellow-horned poppy, sea beet and hoary mullein.

Visiting

Access at all times to the reserve beach and four hides to which visitors are required to walk (passing the holiday chalets) from the public car park. *Only cars with disabled visitors* may drive down and through the reserve gate at the southern end of the chalets.

Facilities

P **G** 30p

The Green, Hunstanton, Norfolk (tel: 048 53 2610).

See advertisements pages 106-107.

Nearest railway station

King's Lynn (12 miles) on the main line from London (Liverpool Street) with an occasional bus link to Snettisham village.

Grey plover

Stour Wood and Copperas Bay, Essex

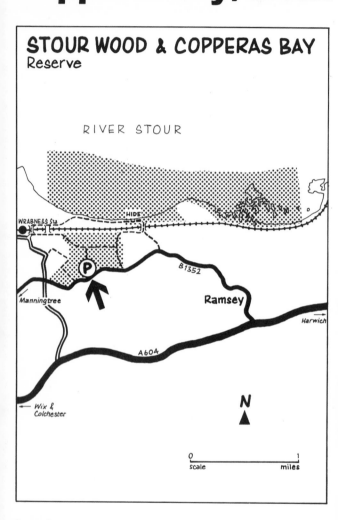

STOUR WOOD & COPPERAS BAY
Reserve

RIVER STOUR

WRABNESS Sta.

HIDE

B1352

Ramsey

Harwich

Manningtree

A604

← Wix &
Colchester

N

0 ——————— 1
scale   miles

Location
Including most of Copperas Bay in the south-east of the Stour estuary west of Harwich, the reserve is entered in Stour Wood off the B1352 road from Manningtree to Ramsey one mile east of Wrabness village. TM/189309.

Tenure
Stour Wood (134 acres) is leased from the Woodland Trust. Most of the foreshore of Copperas Bay and the north part of Copperas Wood are owned (583 acres).

Status
SSSI. Grade 1.

Warden
Russell Leavett, 24 Orchard Close, Great Oakley, Harwich CO12 5AX.

Habitat
The woodland is predominantly of oak and sweet chestnut with extensive chestnut coppice that was worked until the 1970s. Copperas Bay contains mudflats fringed by a little saltmarsh, reedbed and scrubby fields.

Birds
Nightingale, garden warbler, blackcap, lesser whitethroat and both great and lesser spotted woodpeckers inhabit the woods and scrub. A variety of waterfowl feed in the bay in autumn and winter including wigeon, teal, pintail, shelduck, brent geese, redshank, curlew, grey plover and a notably large flock of black-tailed godwits.

Other wildlife
Butcher's broom, yellow archangel and wild service tree occur in Stour Wood with dormice and a colony of white admiral butterflies.

Visiting
Access at all times from two waymarked paths through Stour Wood and ½ mile down to the edge of the estuary where a hide commands a wide view of the bay.

Facilities
P

Parkeston Quay, Harwich, Essex (tel: 0255 506139).

Nearest railway station
Wrabness (1 mile) on the main line from London (Liverpool Street) to Harwich.

Strumpshaw Fen, Norfolk

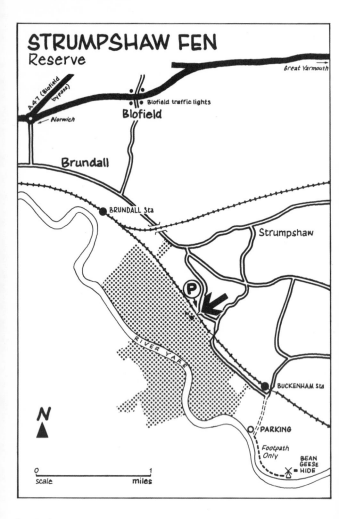

Location

Situated in the Yare Valley in the southern part of the Broads, the reserve is reached from the A47 Norwich to Yarmouth road by turning through Brundall. Beyond the railway bridge turn sharp right and right again into Low Road which leads to the reserve car park. To reach the reception hide, visitors must cross the level-crossing on foot *with care*. TG/342063.

Tenure

128 acres owned and 319 acres leased from W S Key.

Status
SSSI. Grade 1*.

Warden
Mike Blackburn, Staithe Cottage, Low Road, Strumpshaw, Norwich NR13 4HS.

Habitat
A large fen with reed and sedge beds, alder and willow stands, damp woodland and two broads beside the River Yare; also wet grazing marshes.

Birds
Marsh harrier, bearded tit, Cetti's warbler, water rail, great crested grebe, gadwall, tufted duck and reed warbler nest in the fen with redshank, snipe and yellow wagtail in the marshes. Mallard, wigeon and pochard as well as the largest flock of bean geese in Britain occur in winter, notably on the adjacent Buckenham Marshes, when there is a roost of hen harriers in the fen.

Other wildlife
Swallowtail butterflies are occasionally seen as are Chinese water deer, grass snake and several species of dragonflies. Marsh pea, purple loosestrife and marsh sow-thistle flower in the fen.

Visiting
Open all days from 9.00am to 9.00pm or sunset when earlier. A nature trail encircles the fen and includes two hides (one of which is elevated). Another hide with an information annex overlooks the main broad.

From *November to February* a public hide is open at all times by the Buckenham Marshes from which to watch the bean geese and wigeon. It is reached over the level crossing at Buckenham station (TG/349050).

Facilities
P   **IC**   **G** 30p

Augustine Stewart House, 14 Tombland, Norwich (tel: 0603 666071).

Nearest railway station
Buckenham (1 mile) on the line from Norwich (main line from London, Liverpool Street) to Yarmouth.

Surlingham Church Marsh, Norfolk

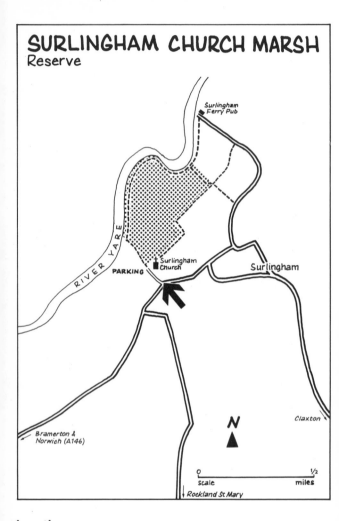

Location
Lying three miles upriver from Strumpshaw Fen (page 110) on the opposite side of the Yare Valley, the reserve is entered on foot from Surlingham church which is reached off the A146 road from Norwich to Lowestoft. TG/306064.

Tenure
214 acres owned.

Status
SSSI. Grade 1*.

Warden
Tony Baker, 2 Chapel Cottages, The Green, Surlingham, Norwich, NR14 7AG.

Habitat
A marsh containing dykes and shallow pools and a mixture of reed, sedge, alder and willow scrub.

Birds
Reed, sedge and grasshopper warblers, gadwall, coot and occasionally pochard and shoveler breed here, while bearded tit, little grebe, kingfisher and Cetti's warbler occur throughout the year. Little ringed plover, green and wood sandpipers visit the marsh on passage and teal, tufted duck, water pipit and hen harrier occur in winter.

Other wildlife
The flora includes water soldier, frogbit, bog bean and marsh orchids. Both noctule and Daubenton's bats may be seen.

Visiting
Access at all times along the waymarked paths from which a hide and reed screens overlook the marsh and pools. Visitors are asked to park with care by the church.

Augustine Stewart House, 14 Tombland, Norwich (tel: 0603 666071).

Nearest railway station
Norwich (6 miles) on the main line from London (Liverpool Street).

Kingfisher

Tetney Marshes, Lincolnshire

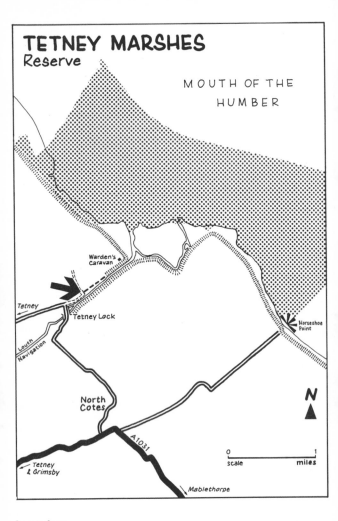

Location
Lying near the mouth of the Humber estuary, the reserve may be entered *on foot* via the locked entrance gate or the riverbank east of Tetney lock. This is east of Tetney village which is on the A1031 south from Cleethorpes. TA/345025.

Tenure
436 acres leased with 2,675 acres held by agreement from adjacent owners.

Status
SSSI. Grade 1*.

Warden
Present from April to August, c/o The Post Office, Tetney, Grimsby, South Humberside.

Habitat
Extensive sandflats bordered by low sand dunes and a wide saltmarsh with creeks.

Birds
The site of one of Britain's largest colonies of little terns which nest at the tide's edge. Shelduck, oystercatcher, ringed plover and redshank also breed. Several migrant species including whimbrel occur and wigeon, teal, brent geese, oystercatcher, grey and golden plovers, bar-tailed godwit and knot flock in winter.

Other wildlife
Grey seals may be seen occasionally.

Visiting
Access at all times. Good views are obtained from the sea wall, especially at high tide. Visitors should avoid the saltmarsh and sand dunes because of the dangerous tides. The little tern colony must not be disturbed.

43 Alexandra Road, Cleethorpes, Humberside (tel: 0472 697472).

Nearest railway station
Cleethorpes (8 miles) on the line from Doncaster or Newark (main line from London, King's Cross).

Little tern

Titchwell Marsh, Norfolk

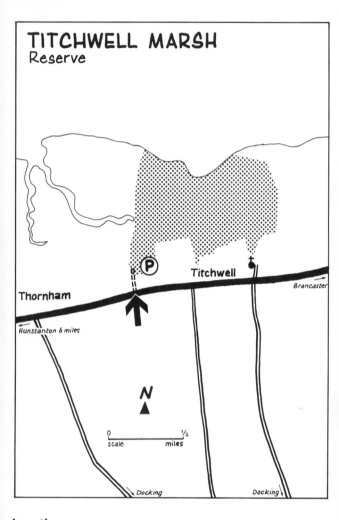

TITCHWELL MARSH Reserve

Thornham

Hunstanton 6 miles

Titchwell

Brancaster

N

0   scale   ½   miles

Docking   Docking

Location
One of a series of nature reserves on the north Norfolk coast, Titchwell is located six miles east of Hunstanton on the A149 road to Brancaster. Enter the reserve car park between Thornham and Titchwell villages. TF/749436.

Tenure
420 acres owned and 90 acres leased from the Crown Estate Commissioners.

Status
SSSI. Grade 1*.

Warden

Norman Sills, Three Horseshoes Cottage, Titchwell, King's Lynn PE31 8BB.

Habitat

Both tidal and freshwater reedbeds, sea aster saltmarsh, brackish and freshwater pools with sand dunes and a shingle beach.

Birds

A growing colony of avocets nests on the enclosed marsh with gadwall, shoveler, black-headed gull and little grebe, while bearded tit, water rail, bittern and marsh harrier are the specialities of the reedbeds. Common and little terns and ringed plover nest on the beach where snow bunting, common scoter and eider may be seen in winter. During that period both brent and pink-footed geese occur regularly and hen harriers roost in the reeds. A range of migrants visit the marsh including black-tailed godwit, curlew sandpiper, black tern and occasional rarities.

Visiting

Access at all times from the car park along the west bank to two hides overlooking the marsh, also the beach with a summer-time hide from which to view the terns. The information centre, RSPB shop and toilets are open from May-September all days except Wednesday, 10.00am-5.00pm; during other months periodically. A picnic area is available.

Facilities

P   WC   IC   &   G 30p   S

The Green, Hunstanton, Norfolk (tel: 048 53 2610).

Camp sites are available at Choseley Farm, 1½ miles south of Titchwell, and in Thornham.

See advertisements pages 107, 118, 119.

Nearest railway station

King's Lynn on the main line from London (Liverpool Street) with bus connection to Hunstanton (6 miles).

Marsh harrier

West Sedgemoor, Somerset

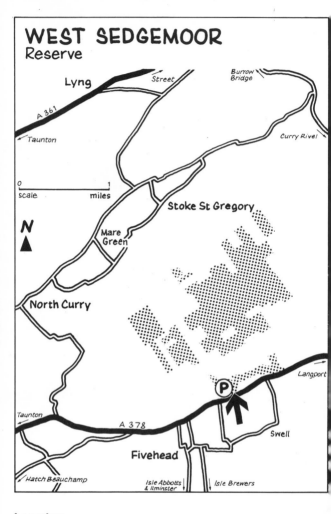

Location
Forming part of the Somerset Levels, this reserve is entered off the A378 road from Taunton to Langport one mile east of Fivehead village. ST/361238.

Tenure
739 acres owned within the much larger moor.

Status
Part SSSI. Grade 1.

Warden

John Humphrey, Hadleigh, White Street, North Curry, near Taunton TA3 6HL.

Habitat

Low-lying wet meadows with intervening droves and ditches and bordered by deciduous woodland on the southern scarp. Winter flooding dries in the spring to enable hay-cutting and the subsequent grazing of cattle.

Birds

Redshank, curlew, snipe, lapwing, black-tailed godwit, yellow wagtail, sedge warbler, whinchat and kestrel nest on the moor where whimbrel are seen regularly on migration. Large flocks of lapwing are joined in winter by golden plover, teal, wigeon and Bewick's swan, depending on the amount of flooding. One of Britain's largest heronries of about 70 pairs is established in Swell Wood where buzzard, blackcap, marsh tit and nightingale breed.

Other wildlife

Marsh marigold, ragged robin and marsh orchid flower in the meadows and water violet in the dykes. Roe deer are often seen.

Visiting

Access at all times to the woodland car park, heronry hide and waymarked path with a viewpoint across the moor. There is another hide at the edge of the moor below.

Facilities

P **G** 30p

The Library, Corporation Street, Taunton, Somerset (tel: 0823 74785).

See advertisement page 124.

Nearest railway station

Taunton (10 miles) on the main line from London (Paddington).

Curlew

Wolves Wood, Suffolk

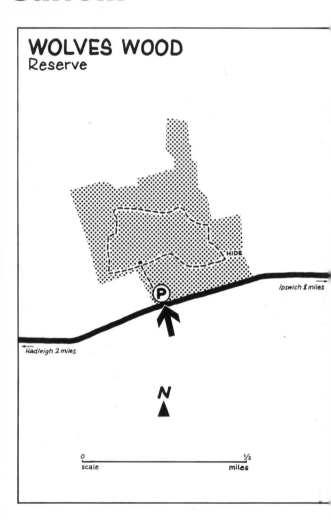

WOLVES WOOD
Reserve

HIDE

Ipswich 8 miles

Hadleigh 2 miles

N

0 ½
scale miles

Location
This wood lies beside the A1071 road to Ipswich two miles east of Hadleigh, in Suffolk farmland. TM/054436.

Tenure
92 acres owned.

Status
SSSI. Grade 1.

Warden
None usually present. Enquiries to Russell Leavett, Stour Wood Reserve (page 109).

Habitat
A mixed deciduous wood of oak, ash, birch, hornbeam, aspen and hazel with an area of coppiced scrub.

Birds
Many nightingales favour the scrub and coppiced rides. Other breeding species include garden warbler, blackcap, chiffchaff, willow warbler, nuthatch, great and lesser spotted woodpeckers, marsh and long-tailed tits, woodcock and occasionally hawfinch.

Other wildlife
Herb paris and yellow archangel indicate this wood's ancient origin.

Visiting
Access at all times from the car park around the waymarked trail (with leaflet).

Facilities
P　　**IC**　　**G** 30p

Town Hall, Princes Street, Ipswich, Suffolk (tel: 0473 58070).

Nearest railway station
Ipswich (8 miles) on the main line from London (Liverpool Street).

Long-tailed tit

SCOTLAND

Balranald, Western Isles

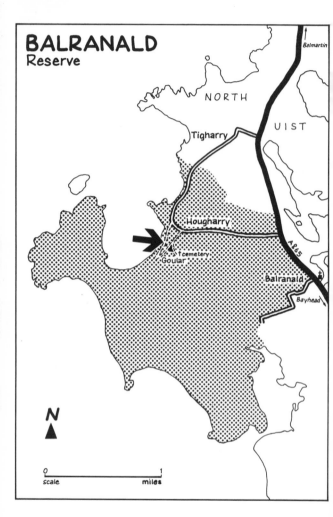

Location
Situated on the Hebridean Island of North Uist, the reserve is reached by turning for Hougharry off the A865 road three miles north of Bayhead. The visitor reception cottage is at Goular. NF/706707.

Tenure
1,625 acres managed by agreement with three neighbouring estates.

Status
SSSI. Grade 1.

Warden
Present from April to August at Goular, near Hougharry, Lochmaddy, North Uist.

Habitat
Sandy beaches and a rocky foreshore are separated from the machair and marshes by sand dunes and there is a shallow, acidic loch. Most of the reserve is worked as crofting land.

Birds
One of the last strongholds of the corncrake and occasionally a pair or two of red-necked phalaropes. Lapwing, snipe, oystercatcher, ringed plover and dunlin nest (at high densities) on the machair while teal, shoveler, gadwall, wigeon and mute swan nest in the marshes. Other breeding birds include little and Arctic terns, twite, wheatear, eider and black guillemot. Whooper swans, greylags and several raptors visit in winter and there is a considerable passage of birds offshore.

Other wildlife
Grey seals breed on the offshore island of Causamul. There is an attractive machair flora.

Visiting
Access at all times. Visitors are asked to keep to the waymarked paths to avoid disturbing ground-nesting birds.

Facilities
IC   **G** 30p

Lochmaddy, Isle of North Uist, Western Isles (tel: 087 63 321).

Camping facilities are available off the reserve.

Ferries travel daily from Uig on Skye to Lochmaddy or from Oban to Lochboisdale on South Uist. Enquiries to Caledonian MacBrayne, Ferry Terminal, Gourock PA19 1QP (tel: 0475 33755).

Red-necked phalarope

Barons Haugh, Strathclyde

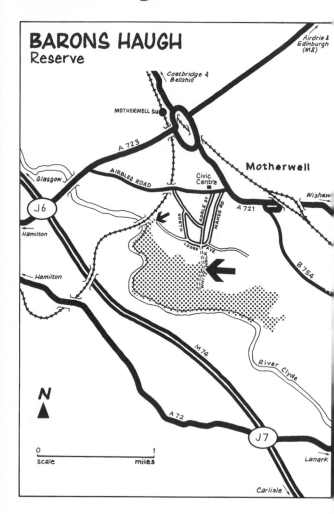

BARONS HAUGH
Reserve

Location
Lying in the Clyde valley ½ mile south of Motherwell town centre, the reserve is entered via Adele Street opposite Motherwell Civic Centre then by a lane leading off North Lodge Avenue. NS/755552.

Tenure
240 acres owned.

Warden
Russell Nisbet, 9 Wisteria Lane, Carluke ML8 5TB.

Habitat

Marsh (the haugh) with permanently flooded areas, woodland, scrub, meadows and parkland beside the River Clyde.

Birds

The haugh attracts wigeon, teal, mallard, pochard and tufted duck in winter as well as over 50 whooper swans. Little grebe, redshank, sedge and grasshopper warblers nest here with king-fisher and common sandpiper along the river. Other breeding birds include garden warbler, tree pipit and whinchat.

Other wildlife

Red squirrels and roe deer occasionally are seen.

Visiting

Access at all times. Two hides overlook the haugh and there is a one-hour walk around it.

Facilities

The Library, Hamilton Road, Motherwell, Strathclyde (tel: 0698 64414).

Nearest railway station

Motherwell (1½ miles) on the line from Glasgow Central to Edinburgh.

Whooper swan

Birsay Moors and Cottasgarth, Orkney

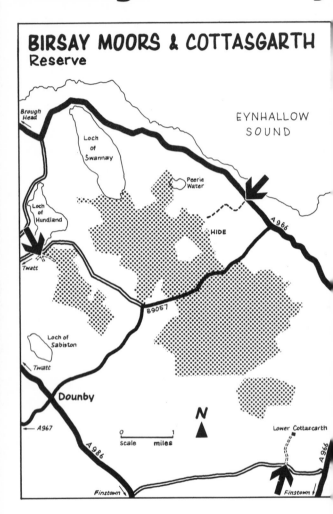

BIRSAY MOORS & COTTASGARTH
Reserve

Brough Head

EYNHALLOW SOUND

Loch of Swannay

Peerie Water

A 966

Loch of Hundland

HIDE

Twatt

B9057

Loch of Sabiston

Twatt

Dounby

N

← A967

A 986

0   1
scale   miles

Lower Cottascarth

A 966

Finstown

Finstown

Location
Situated in the north of the Mainland of Orkney, this large reserve may be enjoyed from a number of points – see below.

Tenure
3,564 acres owned and 2,217 acres leased from two owners.

Status
SSSI. Grade 1.

Warden

Occasionally present from April to August. Enquiries to RSPB Orkney Officer (page 7).

Habitat

Undulating heather moorland on the Old Red Sandstone with blanket bog, marshy areas and streams.

Birds

An unusually high density of hen harriers nest here with a few merlins and ground-nesting kestrels. Small colonies of both great and Arctic skuas as well as great and lesser black-backed gulls, herring gulls and common gulls are also present. Other breeding species include oystercatcher, golden plover, curlew, dunlin, stonechat, wheatear and short-eared owl with several species of ducks.

Other wildlife

The Orkney vole is common. The *Dee of Durkadale* is rich in orchids and sedges.

Visiting

Access at all times. *Cottasgarth* is reached along a track by turning left off the A966 road three miles north of Finstown, just north of Norseman Garage (HY/368187). It has a small hide providing good views of the moorland birds especially hen harriers. A hide at *Burgar Hill*, by the wind generators, is signposted from the A966 at Evie (HY/358266). The *Birsay Moors* may be viewed from the B9057 road from Dounby to Georth. *Dee of Durkadale* is reached by turning right along the rough track at the south end of Loch Hundland to the ruined farm of Durkadale (HY/293252). Please close gates.

Facilities

G to Orkney Reserves 60p

Orkney Tourist Board, 6 Broad Street, Kirkwall (tel: 0856 2856).

Ferries run daily from Scrabster in Caithness to Stromness on Mainland Orkney. Enquiries to P&O Ferries, Orkney and Shetland Services, PO Box 5, Aberdeen AB9 8DL (tel: 0224 572615).

Orkney vole

Copinsay, Orkney

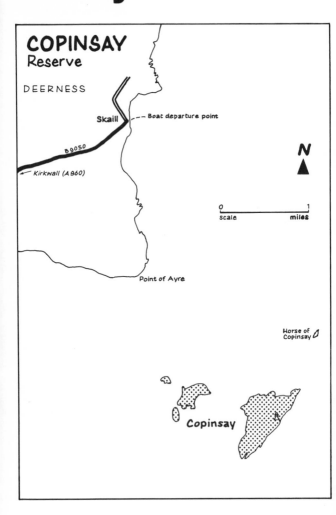

Location
An island 7 miles off the east coast of Mainland Orkney near Skaill.
HY/610010.

Tenure
375 acres owned.

Status
SSSI. Grade 2.

Warden
None present. Enquiries to RSPB Orkney Officer (page 7).

Habitat
An island of Old Red Sandstone with almost a mile of sheer cliffs, also rocky shores connecting it to islets.

Birds
Very large cliff-nesting colonies of kittiwake, guillemot, razorbill and fulmar with some shags, puffins, black guillemots and cormorants. Both great and lesser black-backed gulls, Arctic tern, rock dove, eider, twite, raven and occasionally corncrake also breed. A good variety of passage migrants can be seen in spring and autumn during periods of easterly winds.

Other wildlife
There is a fine colony of oyster plant on the beach.

Visiting
Access at all times by taking day-trips to the island by boat from Skaill (contact S Foubister – tel: 085 674 252). Excellent views may be obtained of the cliff-nesting birds from several points but visitors are asked to *take great care*.

Facilities
G to Orkney Reserves 60p

For ferry connections and accommodation see page 131.

Seabird cliff

Culbin Sands, Highland/Grampian

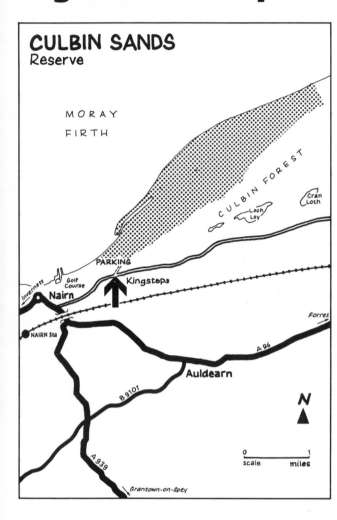

CULBIN SANDS
Reserve

MORAY FIRTH

CULBIN FOREST

Cran Loch

Loch Loy

Inverness

Golf Course

PARKING

Kingsteps

Nairn

NAIRN Sta

B 9101

Auldearn

A 96

Forres

A 939

Grantown-on-Spey

N

0 scale 1 miles

Location
On the southern shore of the Moray Firth, this reserve is entered at Kingsteps one mile east of Nairn along the minor road past the golf course. NH/901573.

Tenure
2,130 acres leased from two owners.

Status
SSSI. Grade 1.

Warden

None present. Enquiries to RSPB Scottish Office (page 7).

Habitat

A long stretch of foreshore comprising sandflats, saltmarsh, shingle bars and spits, backed by the largest sand dune system in Britain, which is almost entirely afforested.

Birds

Winter flocks of bar-tailed godwit, oystercatcher, knot, dunlin, ringed plover, redshank and curlew with mallard, shelduck, red-breasted merganser and greylag geese. Large concentrations of both common and velvet scoters with long-tailed ducks congregate offshore. Breeding birds include oystercatcher, ringed plover, redshank, a few eider, and little and common terns.

Visiting

Access at all times to the beach. Visitors should beware of the tides and creeks.

62 High Street, Nairn, Highland (tel: 0667 52753).

Nearest railway station

Nairn (1 ½ miles) on the line from Inverness to Aberdeen.

Scoter

Fetlar, Shetland

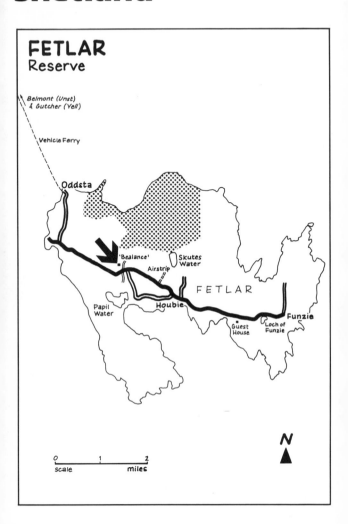

FETLAR
Reserve

Belmont (Unst)
& Gutcher (Yell)

Vehicle Ferry

Oddsta

'Bealance'   Skutes
Airstrip   Water

F E T L A R

Papil
Water   Houbie   Funzie

Guest   Loch of
House   Funzie

0   1   2
scale   miles

N

Location
Being the smallest of the three inhabited northern islands of
Shetland, Fetlar is reached by public car ferry from Yell and Unst.
Another ferry connects Yell to the mainland of Shetland.

Tenure
1,700 acres of the northern part of the island is a reserve by
agreement with the owners.

Status
SSSI. Grade 1. A Statutory Bird Sanctuary.

Warden

Present from April to September at Bealance, Fetlar ZE2 9DJ. Otherwise enquiries to RSPB Shetland Officer (page 7).

Habitat

Most of the reserve consists of grassy heathland on serpentine rock, encompassing the summits of Vord Hill and Stackaberg, and bordered by high sea cliffs and boulder shores to the north and crofting areas in the south. The heather moor and blanket bog of the west of Fetlar contrasts with some dry heath in the east. Otherwise there are numerous lochs, pools and marshy areas on the island.

Birds

The reserve is famous for Britain's only pair of snowy owls that nested here from 1969-75, since when only female owls have been resident, Fetlar's breeding birds include Manx shearwater, storm petrel, shag, eider, red-throated diver, golden plover, dunlin, snipe, curlew, raven, twite and an important population of whimbrel. Red-necked phalaropes may be watched from the road feeding on the Loch of Funzie. Many passage migrants including rarities occur in spring and autumn.

Other wildlife

Common and grey seals and otters frequent the coast.

Visiting

Visitors are welcome to the island all year, but the reserve and sanctuary may not be entered in summer other than by arrangement with the warden, who escorts parties to view the snowy owls. Bealance is signposted 2½ miles from the Oddsta ferry terminal (HU/604916). Visitors are asked not to disturb the breeding birds and to respect the property of farmers and crofters.

Facilities

G to Shetland Reserves 50p

Shetland Tourist Organisation, Market Cross, Lerwick, Shetland (tel: 3434). There is a guest house on Fetlar.

Shetland may be reached by **car ferry** from Aberdeen or Orkney or by **air** from Edinburgh, Aberdeen, Inverness and Orkney. Ferry enquiries to P&O Ferries, Orkney and Shetland Services, PO Box 5, Aberdeen AB9 8DL (tel: 0224 572615).

A **bus** from Lerwick connects with the public ferry but does not cross to Fetlar. Advanced booking of vehicles for the ferry is *essential* (tel: Burravoe 259/268).

Fowlsheugh, Grampian

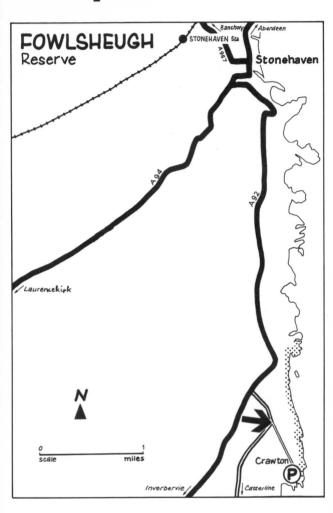

Location
The small cliff-top car park for this reserve is at Crawton which is signposted from the A92 road to Inverbervie three miles south of Stonehaven. NO/876805.

Tenure
1½ miles of cliff owned.

Status
SSSI. Grade 1*.

Warden
None present. Enquiries to RSPB Scottish Office (page 7).

Habitat
Old Red Sandstone grass-topped cliffs with nooks and ledges.

Birds
Very large colonies of guillemot, razorbill and kittiwake with smaller numbers of fulmar, herring gull, shag and puffin nest on the cliffs. Eiders occur offshore.

Other wildlife
Seals occasionally are seen.

Visiting
Access at all times along the cliff-top path from which the seabirds may be viewed well at several points. Visitors are warned to *take care* at the cliff-edge.

Facilities
P

The Square, Stonehaven, Grampian (tel: 0569 62806).

Nearest railway station
Stonehaven (4½ miles) on the line from Perth to Aberdeen.

Razorbill

Handa, Highland

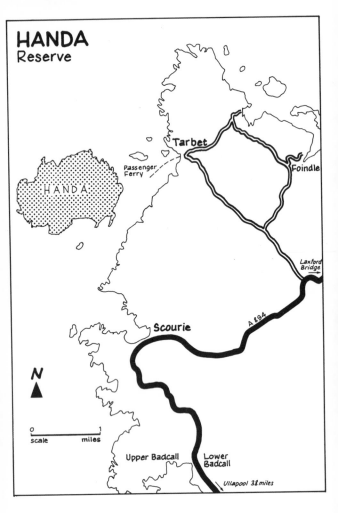

Location
This large island lies off the coast of the Torridon district in the north-west of the Scottish Highlands. It is reached by boat from Tarbet off the A894 road from Laxford Bridge to Scourie. NC/130480.

Tenure
766 acres managed by agreement with the owner, Dr J Balfour.

Status
SSSI. Grade 2.

Warden
Present from April to August, c/o Mrs A Munro, Tarbet, near Lairg IV27 4SS.

Habitat
The island rises from sandy bays to high sandstone cliffs and stacks with an interior of rough pasture, peat bogs and a few lochans.

Birds
Spectacular numbers of guillemot, razorbill, puffin, kittiwake and fulmar nest on the cliffs with shag and great black-backed gull. Growing colonies of both Arctic and great skuas inhabit the moor with red-throated diver on the lochans and oystercatcher, ringed plover and eider on the beaches. Many species such as green-shank and whimbrel occur on migration.

Other wildlife
Various species of whale and dolphin are seen offshore as well as grey seal. Limestone bugle flowers.

Visiting
A boat service to the island operates from Tarbet daily *except Sunday* between 1 April and 10 September. Visitors are asked to keep to the waymarked path and to take *special care* on the cliff-top from which the seabirds can be viewed well.

RSPB members may stay in the island bothy by arrangement with the RSPB Scottish Office (page 7).

Facilities
G 30p

Lochinver, Highland (tel: 057 14 330).

Nearest railway station
Lairg (40 miles) on the line from Inverness to Thurso.

Eider

Hobbister, Orkney

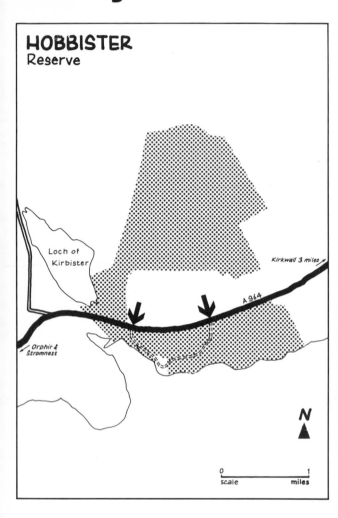

HOBBISTER
Reserve

Loch of
Kirbister

Kirkwall 3 miles

A964

Orphir &
Stromness

N

0   1
scale   miles

Location
Lying either side of the A964 road from Kirkwall to Stromness near the village of Orphir on Orkney Mainland, the reserve may be entered along a track at HY/396070 or a minor road at HY/381068.

Tenure
1,875 acres leased from Highland Park Distillery Ltd.

Status
Part SSSI.

Warden

Only occasionally present. Enquiries to RSPB Orkney Office (page 7).

Habitat

Predominantly heather moorland with bogs and fen and drained by the Swartaback Burn. Also low sea-cliffs above the sandy Waulkmill Bay and a small area of saltmarsh.

Birds

The typical Orkney moorland species of hen harrier, short-eared owl, merlin, red grouse, curlew, snipe, red-throated diver and twite breed on the moorland with colonies of lesser black-backed and common gulls. Fulmar, raven, eider, red-breasted merganser and black guillemot nest on the coast where divers and sea-ducks may be seen at other times.

Other wildlife

Round-leaved sundew, butterwort and bog asphodel flower in the bogs.

Visiting

Access at all times but visitors are asked not to disturb the breeding divers and birds of prey. Waulkmill Bay provides some good birdwatching outside the breeding season.

Facilities

G to Orkney Reserves 60p

For ferry connections and accommodation see page 131.

Short-eared owl

Insh Marshes, Highland

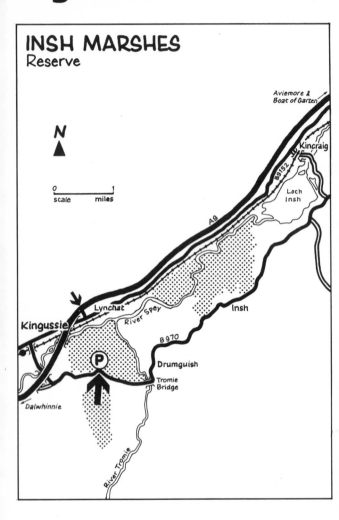

INSH MARSHES
Reserve

N

0 — 1
scale — miles

Aviemore &
Boat of Garten

Kincraig

B9152

Loch
Insh

A9

Lynchat

River Spey

Insh

Kingussie

B970

Drumguish

P

Tromie
Bridge

Dalwhinnie

River Tromie

Location
Situated on Speyside between Kingussie and Loch Insh, the reserve reception and car park is entered off the B970 road to Insh village 1½ miles from Kingussie. NH/775998.

Tenure
1,607 acres owned and 315 acres leased from adjacent owners.

Status
Mostly SSSI. Grade 1.

Warden

Zul Bhatia, Ivy Cottage, Insh, Kingussie PH21 1NT.

Habitat

Extensive marshes in the floodplain of the upper River Spey which usually flood in winter. Also sedge meadows with pools and willow scrub bordered by birch with juniper woodland from which extends some moorland into the foothills of the Cairngorms.

Birds

The wetland breeding species include wigeon, teal, shoveler, tufted duck, goldeneye, (native) greylag, snipe, curlew, redshank and both sedge and grasshopper warblers. Woodcock, great spotted woodpecker, tree pipit, redstart and occasionally pied flycatcher nest in the woodland with dipper and grey wagtail on the burns. Osprey, hen harrier and buzzard are seen regularly. Large numbers of whooper swans visit the marshes in winter when greylag and pink-footed geese pass on migration.

Other wildlife

Otter and roe deer are present. Scotch argus is a notable butterfly.

Visiting

Open on all days *except Tuesday* 9.00am to 9.00pm or sunset when earlier. Two hides overlooking the marshes are reached along waymarked woodland paths.

Facilities

P   **IC**   **G** 30p

King Street, Kingussie, Highland (tel: 054 02 297).

Nearest railway station

Kingussie (1½ miles) on the main line from Edinburgh to Inverness.

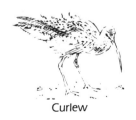

Curlew

Inversnaid, Central

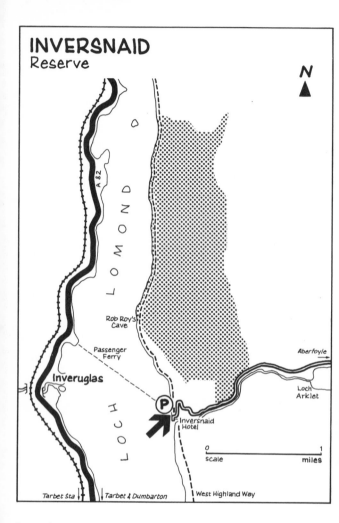

INVERSNAID
Reserve

A 82

LOMOND

Rob Roy's
Cave

Passenger
Ferry

Inveruglas

LOCH

P

Inversnaid
Hotel

Aberfoyle

Loch
Arklet

0 scale 1 miles

Tarbet Sta | Tarbet & Dumbarton | West Highland Way

N

Location
Lying on the east side of Loch Lomond, this Trossachs reserve is approached by an unclassified road by taking the B829 west from Aberfoyle. NN/337088.

Tenure
923 acres owned.

Status
Part SSSI. Grade 2.

Warden

Mike Trubridge, Garrison Cottage, Inversnaid, Aberfoyle, Central FK8 3TU.

Habitat

The ground rises steeply from Loch Lomond through deciduous woodland to a craggy ridge, beyond which lies moorland of grass and heather. Several mountain burns descend to the loch.

Birds

The resident woodland birds are joined by summer migrants such as wood warbler, redstart, pied flycatcher and tree pipit. Buzzards nest in the crags and in the woods and blackcock frequent the lower slopes. Dipper, grey wagtail and common sandpiper breed on the loch shore and along the burns. The loch itself is a migration route especially for wildfowl and waders.

Other wildlife

The bryophyte and lichen communities are exceptional. Badger, feral goat and both red and roe deer are present.

Visiting

Access at all times along the long distance footpath, the West Highland Way, which follows the loch shore and offers a pleasant woodland walk. There is a car park at the road end by Inversnaid Hotel where toilets are available during the summer. A pedestrian ferry crosses from Inveruglas on the west bank of Loch Lomond, mainly in summer: telephone Inversnaid Hotel (087 786 223) for arrangements.

Facilities

P   WC

Main Street, Aberfoyle, Central (tel: 087 72 352).

Nearest railway station

Stirling (35 miles) on the line from Glasgow to Perth.

Buzzard

Ken-Dee Marshes, Dumfries and Galloway

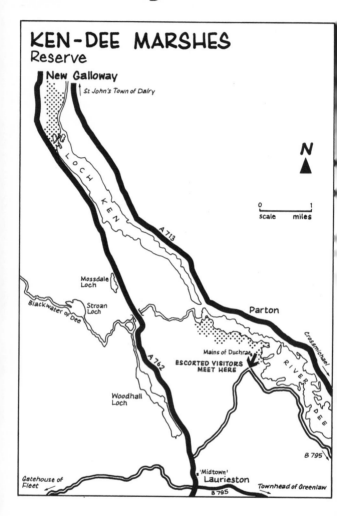

KEN-DEE MARSHES
Reserve

New Galloway

St John's Town of Dalry

LOCH KEN

A 713

N

0 — scale — 1 — miles

Mossdale Loch

Blackwater of Dee

Stroan Loch

Parton

Crossmichael

Mains of Duchrae
ESCORTED VISITORS MEET HERE

RIVER DEE

A 762

Woodhall Loch

B 795

Gatehouse of Fleet

'Midtown'
Laurieston

Townhead of Greenlaw

B 795

Location
Lying in the valley of the River Dee between New Galloway and Castle Douglas, the reserve occurs in two parts beside and upstream of Loch Ken.

Tenure
326 acres leased from several owners.

Status
SSSI. Grade 1.

Warden
Ray Hawley, Midtown, Laurieston, near Castle Douglas DG7 2PP.

Habitat
Marshes and meadows of the River Dee floodplain bordered by hillside farmland and deciduous woods.

Birds
In winter some 300 Greenland white-fronted geese visit the valley together with greylag geese, wigeon, pintail, teal, mallard, shoveler, goosander and whooper swans. Hen harriers, merlins, peregrines and buzzards hunt the area. The marshland breeding birds include redshank, great crested grebe, teal and shoveler while redstart, pied flycatcher and willow tit nest in the woodland. Crossbills and siskins occur locally.

Other wildlife
Red squirrels and roe deer are quite plentiful and otters are recorded occasionally.

Visiting
There is no access to the reserve other than by *written arrangement* with the warden who escorts parties (charge: £2 to non-members). However, good views are obtained from the A762 road and its offshoots on the west of the valley, as from the A713 on the opposite side. Visitors are asked to park at the roadside *with care* and not to obstruct local traffic.

Markethill, Castle Douglas, Dumfries and Galloway (tel: 0556 2611).

See advertisements page 150.

Nearest railway station
Dumfries which is connected by bus service to Castle Douglas (6 miles).

Merlin

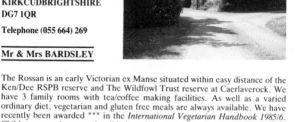

Killiecrankie, Tayside

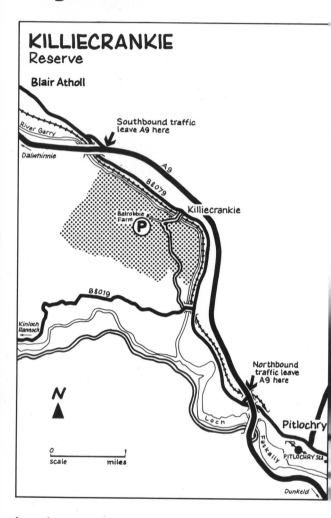

KILLIECRANKIE
Reserve

Blair Atholl

River Garry

Southbound traffic
leave A9 here

Dalwhinnie

A9

B8079

Killiecrankie

Balrobbie
Farm

P

B8019

Kinloch
Rannoch

Northbound
traffic leave
A9 here

N

Loch

Faskally

Pitlochry

PITLOCHRY Stn.

Dunkeld

0   scale   1   miles

Location
Lying in Highlands scenery, this reserve is reached by turning off the main A9 road just north of Pitlochry and proceeding to Killiecrankie on the B8079 road, then taking the minor road south-westwards to the warden's house at NN/907627.

Tenure
950 acres leased from G S Murdoch.

Status
SSSI. Partly Grade 1.

Warden

Martin Robinson, Balrobbie Farm, Killiecrankie, Pitlochry PH16 5LJ.

Habitat

Sessile oakwoods also containing birch, ash, wych elm and alder rise from the gorge of the River Garry to a plateau of pastureland. Above this a zone of birchwood ascends steeply through crags to a ridge of heather moorland.

Birds

Wood warbler, redstart, tree pipit and occasionally pied flycatcher nest in the woodland as well as garden warbler, crossbill, sparrowhawk, buzzard and both green and great spotted woodpeckers. Black grouse and whinchat frequent the moorland fringe and raven and kestrel inhabit the crags. Both golden eagle and peregrine are seen occasionally.

Other wildlife

Red squirrels and roe deer are plentiful. A rich reserve flora includes yellow mountain saxifrage, globe flower, grass of Parnassus and several species of orchids.

Visiting

Access to the waymarked trail at all times. Visitors may be escorted by written arrangement with the warden (charge: £1 to non-members).

Facilities

P

i

22 Atholl Road, Pitlochry, Tayside (tel: 0796 2215).

Nearest railway station

Pitlochry (4 miles) on the main line from Edinburgh to Inverness.

Wood warbler

Loch Garten, Highland

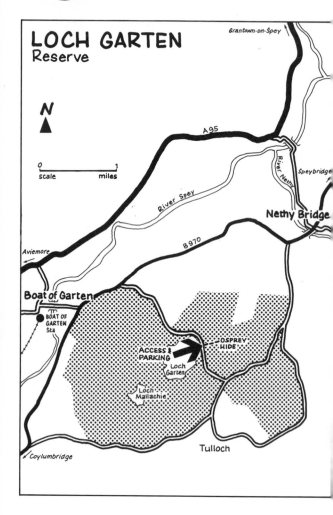

Location
Renowned for its osprey observation post, this Speyside reserve comprises a large portion of the Abernethy Forest east of Boat of Garten from which it is signposted off the B970 road to Nethybridge. Access is beside Loch Garten itself at NH/978184.

Tenure
2,949 acres owned.

Status
SSSI. Grade 1*. The osprey nest site is within a Statutory Bird Sanctuary.

Warden

Stewart Taylor, Grianan, Nethybridge PH25 3EF.

Habitat

A very important remnant of the once more extensive Scots pine forest of the Scottish Highlands with an understorey of juniper in places. Also forest bogs, two lochs, some crofting land and a fringe of heather moorland.

Birds

In addition to the regular nesting pair of ospreys, the reserve has a characteristic breeding birds community of crested tit, Scottish crossbill, capercaillie, black grouse, redstart, siskin and sparrow-hawk with teal, wigeon and little grebe on the lochs. Greylag, goldeneye and goosander resort to Loch Garten in winter.

Other wildlife

The pinewood plants of chickweed wintergreen, bilberry and creeping lady's tresses occur. Resident mammals include red squirrel, pine marten, wildcat and both red and roe deer.

Visiting

Provided the ospreys are nesting, the observation post with RSPB shop is open daily from mid-April to August from 10.00am to 8.00pm. Powerful binoculars and telescopes allow close views of the ospreys on their eyrie. Otherwise the reserve is accessible at all times but visitors are asked to keep to the forest tracks and paths. High fire risk – please do not light matches.

Facilities

P   IC   S   &   G 30p

i

Boat Hotel Car Park, Boat of Garten, Highland (tel: 047 983 307).

A free tourist booklet about the area is available from the warden for a large SAE.

See advertisement page 150.

Nearest railway station

Carrbridge (8 miles) on the main line from Edinburgh to Inverness. The Strathspey Railway links this to Boat of Garten.

Loch Gruinart, Islay, Strathclyde

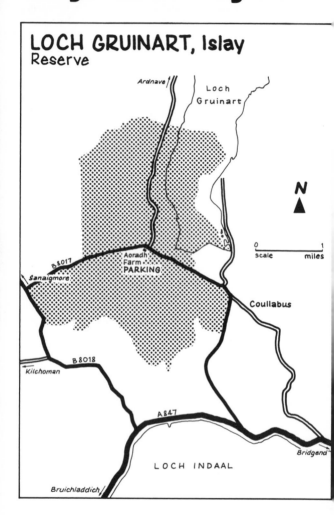

LOCH GRUINART, Islay
Reserve

Location
Situated in the north of the Hebridean island of Islay, the reserve lies on the south and west of Loch Gruinart and straddles the B8017 road west of Bridgend.

Tenure
4,087 acres owned.

Status
Partly SSSI. Grade 1*.

Warden
Bushmills Cottages, Gruinart, Bridgend, Isle of Islay PA44 7PP.

Habitat
Improved and rough pasture 'flats' with saltmarsh at the head of the tidal Loch Gruinart; also moorland with patches of woodland and hill lochs.

Birds
The major feeding and roosting site in the British Isles for the Greenland race of barnacle geese, numbering up to 20,000 when they overwinter on Islay from October to April. Also large flocks of white-fronted geese. Hen harrier, buzzard and short-eared owl breed and may be seen also in winter with golden eagle, peregrine, merlin, whooper swan and chough. Teal, redshank, snipe, curlew and stonechat nest.

Other wildlife
Otter, grey and common seals and both red and roe deer are often to be seen.

Visiting
Good birdwatching may be obtained from the B8017 and the minor road north to Ardnave. Cars may be parked at Aoradh Farm (NR/276673) to avoid blocking the roadside passing-places. Visitors are asked not to enter the fields to avoid disturbing the geese or livestock.

Facilities
P

Bowmore, Isle of Islay, Strathclyde (tel: 049 681 254).

See advertisements page 151.

Ferries cross daily from Kennacraig, on Kintyre, to Port Ellen. Enquiries to Caledonian MacBrayne, Ferry Terminal, Gourock PA19 1QP (tel: 0475 33755).

Air service from Glasgow to Port Ellen. Enquiries to Loganair (tel: 041 889 3181).

Loch of Kinnordy, Tayside

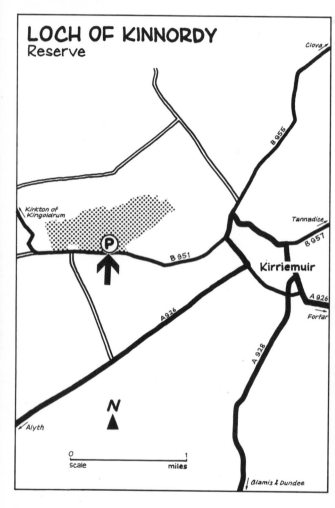

Location
Situated off the B951 road one mile west of Kirriemuir. NO/361539.

Tenure
200 acres owned.

Status
SSSI. Grade 2.

Warden

Present from April to August at The Flat, Kinnordy Home Farm, Kirriemuir DD8 5ER.

Habitat

A freshwater marsh with varying amounts of open water, containing willow and alder scrub, fringed by woodland and set in a farming landscape.

Birds

Mallard, teal, shoveler, tufted duck, gadwall and ruddy duck nest as well as sedge warbler, reed bunting, redshank and a large colony of black-headed gulls. Sparrowhawk and long-eared owl occur and greenshank, ruff, osprey and black-necked grebe are often seen on migration. A large roost of greylag geese gathers in winter with a variety of ducks and hunting short-eared owl and hen harrier.

Visiting

Open on all days from April to August, and on *Sundays only* from September to November. Hours: 9.00am to 9.00pm or sunset when earlier. The reserve is *closed* from December to March. Paths lead from a small car park to the hides.

Facilities

P

i

Bank Street, Kirriemuir, Tayside (tel: 0575 74097).

Nearest railway station

Dundee (18 miles) on the main line from Edinburgh to Aberdeen.

Shoveler

Loch of Spiggie, Shetland

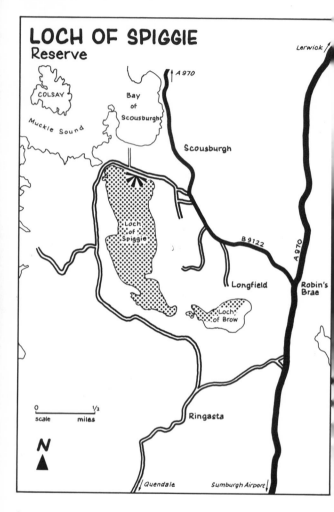

Location
Situated near the southern end of mainland Shetland, the reserve is approached by turning off the B9122 road near Scousburgh which is west of the A970 from Lerwick four miles north of Sumburgh airport.

Tenure
284 acres owned.

Status
SSSI. Grade 2.

Warden
None regularly present. Enquiries to RSPB Shetland Officer (page 7).

Habitat
A shallow freshwater loch separated from the sea by sand dunes and from the neighbouring Loch of Brow (partly in the reserve) by a marsh.

Birds
Teal, shelduck, oystercatcher and curlew nest in the area while the loch is often used for bathing by Arctic terns, both great and Arctic skuas and kittiwakes. Long-tailed ducks gather to display on the loch in spring. As many as 300 whooper swans winter here regularly as well as greylag, tufted duck, pochard, goldeneye and wigeon.

Other wildlife
Otters are resident.

Visiting
The reserve may not be entered, but good views of the loch are obtained from the minor road at the north end HU/373176. Care should be taken not to impede other road-users.

Shetland Tourist Organisation, Market Cross, Lerwick, Shetland (tel: 3434).

See page 136 for details of **ferries** to Shetland. A bus from Lerwick to Sumburgh can disembark passengers at Robin's Brae, two miles from the reserve.

Kittiwake

Loch of Strathbeg, Grampian

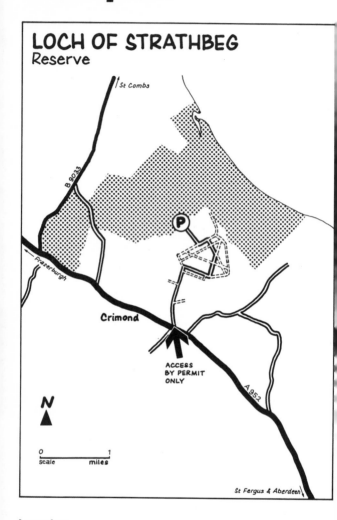

Location
Lying between the sea and the A952 Peterhead to Fraserburgh road near the village of Crimond, the reserve may *only* be entered by permit (see below). NK/063564.

Tenure
65 acres owned and 2,000 acres leased from several owners.

Status
SSSI. Partly Grade 1.

Warden
Jim Dunbar, The Lythe, Crimonmogate, Lonmay, Fraserburgh AB4 4UB.

Habitat
A large shallow loch on the Aberdeenshire coast, separated from the sea by wide sand dunes and bordered by freshwater fen and marsh, saltmarsh, woodland and farmland.

Birds
Major concentrations of wintering whooper swan, tufted duck, pochard, goldeneye and both greylag and pink-footed geese gather on and around the loch which also serves as a migratory staging post. There are also red-breasted merganser, goosander, mallard, wigeon and occasionally smew. Breeding birds include eider, shelduck, tufted duck, water rail and sedge warbler. A large colony of Sandwich terns nests on artificial islands in one bay.

Other wildlife
Roe deer are seen frequently and badgers and otters are present. Lesser butterfly orchids and coral root orchids occur.

Visiting
Because access is across MoD property it is *essential* to obtain a permit (charge £1 to non-members) from the warden before visiting. Three hides overlook the bays and islands in the north-west part of the loch and there is a boardwalk through fen woodland from the information centre.

Facilities
P　**IC**　**WC**　**G** 30p

Saltoun Square, Fraserburgh, Grampian (tel: 0346 28315).

Nearest railway station
Aberdeen (40 miles) on the main line from Edinburgh.

Badger

Lochwinnoch, Strathclyde

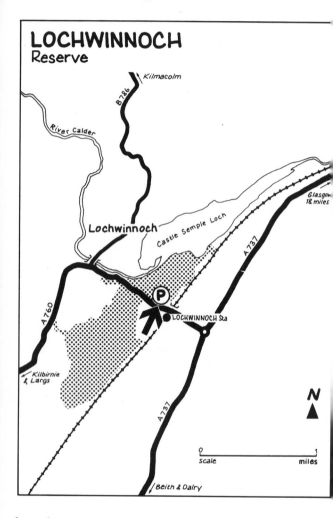

LOCHWINNOCH
Reserve

Location
The nature centre and reserve lie off the A760 road from Largs to Paisley, ½ mile east of Lochwinnoch. NS/359581.

Tenure
388 acres leased from Strathclyde Regional Council.

Status
SSSI.

Warden

John Hawell, Lochwinnoch Nature Centre, Largs Road, Lochwinnoch, Strathclyde (tel: 0505 842663).

Habitat

This reserve comprises the shallow Barr Loch and the sedge marsh of Aird Meadow together with some alder and willow scrub and deciduous woodland.

Birds

Great crested and little grebes, snipe, shoveler, pochard, tufted duck, dipper and a colony of black-headed gulls nest as well as grasshopper and sedge warblers. Several waders occur on passage. In winter whooper swan, greylag, goosander, wigeon, teal, pochard and coot frequent the loch. Kestrel, sparrowhawk and occasionally peregrine may be seen throughout the year.

Other wildlife

Marsh marigold, yellow water-lily and valerian flower. Roe deer occur.

Visiting

The reserve is open on all days from 9.00am to 9.00pm or sunset when earlier. The nature trail incorporates three hides overlooking marsh and open water. The Centre, with observation tower and RSPB gift shop, is open from 10.00am to 5.15pm daily. Charge to non-members: 60p.

Facilities

P   IC   WC   S   &   G 50p

Town Hall, Abbey Close, Paisley, Strathclyde (tel: 041 889 0711).

Nearest railway station

Lochwinnoch (¼ mile) on the line from Glasgow Central to Ayr.

Sparrowhawk

The Loons, Orkney

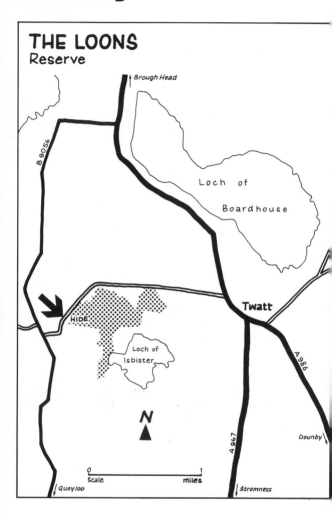

Location
Situated in the north of mainland Orkney beside the Loch of Isbister, the reserve is approached along the minor road from the A986 three miles north of Dounby.

Tenure
139 acres owned.

Status
SSSI.

Warden
None regularly present. Enquiries to RSPB Orkney Officer (page 7).

Habitat
A marsh within a basin of Old Red Sandstone hills, containing old peat workings and bordered by a loch.

Birds
Teal, shoveler, wigeon, pintail, red-breasted merganser, snipe and redshank breed here as well as colonies of common and black-headed gulls and Arctic terns. Corncrakes occur occasionally. A regular flock of Greenland white-fronted geese and several species of ducks visit it in winter.

Other wildlife
Grass of Parnassus, alpine meadow-rue and several species of orchids flower here. Otters occur.

Visiting
Access at all times to the hide on the west side (HY/246242) but the reserve itself may not be entered to avoid disturbance.

Facilities
G to Orkney Reserves 60p

For **ferry** connections and accommodation see page 131.

Grass of Parnassus

Lumbister, Shetland

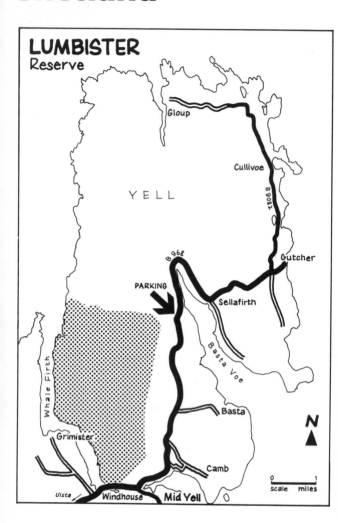

Location
Occupies the west side of the island of Yell between Whale Firth and the A968 road to Gutcher.

Tenure
4,000 acres owned.

Warden
Occasionally present during summer. Enquiries to RSPB Shetland Officer (page 7).

Habitat

Extensive, undulating moorland of heather and bog broken by many water-bodies as well as a steep gorge leading to the rugged grass-topped cliffs and rocky shore of Whale Firth.

Birds

Red-throated diver, red-breasted merganser and eider nest on the lochs while merlin and both Arctic and great skuas breed on the moorland with golden plover, curlew, dunlin and twite. Raven, wheatear, rock dove, puffin and black guillemot nest on the cliffs.

Other wildlife

Otters are common and both grey and common seals may be seen offshore. Lesser twayblades grow in the bogs and juniper and roseroot in the gorge.

Visiting

Good views may be obtained from the A968 road. Pedestrian access is gained from the lay-by four miles north of Mid Yell (HU/509974) but visitors are asked to take care not to disturb the divers and other breeding birds.

Facilities

G to Shetland Reserves 50p

Shetland Tourist Organisation, Market Cross, Lerwick, Shetland (tel: 3434).

A car **ferry** operates between mainland Shetland and the island of Yell. See also page 136.

Red-throated diver

Marwick Head, Orkney

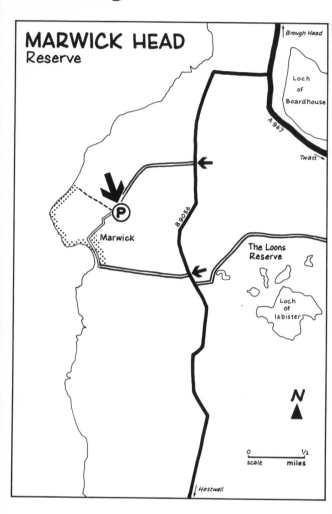

Location
Lies on the west coast of mainland Orkney north of Marwick Bay to which a minor road runs from the B9056. HY/232249.

Tenure
One mile of cliffs owned.

Status
SSSI. Grade 1.

Warden
None present. Enquiries to RSPB Orkney Officer (page 7).

Habitat
Sheer cliffs of Old Red Sandstone, rising almost to 300ft, on which there are numerous ledges for nesting seabirds. Part of the rocky bay of Marwick and some wet meadowland are also within the reserve.

Birds
The most spectacular seabird breeding colony on mainland Orkney, holding very large populations of guillemot and kittiwake. Razorbill, fulmar, rock dove, raven, peregrine and wheatear also nest here.

Other wildlife
Thrift, sea campion and spring squill provide a fine show of flowers. Both grey and common seals may be seen.

Visiting
Access at all times by walking from the car park at Cumlaquoy (HY/232252), alternatively from the road end at Marwick Bay (HY/229242). The seabirds may be viewed well from the cliff-top, but visitors are cautioned to *take great care*.

Facilities
P   **G** to Orkney Reserves 60p

Orkney Tourist Board, 6 Broad Street, Kirkwall (tel: 0856 2856).

For details of **ferries** to Orkney see page 131.

Guillemot

Mull of Galloway, Dumfries and Galloway

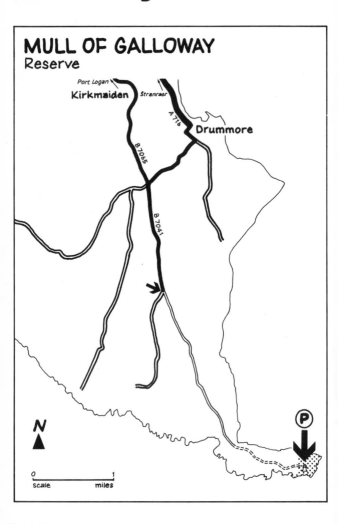

MULL OF GALLOWAY
Reserve

Port Logan
Kirkmaiden
Stranraer
A 716
Drummore
B 7065
B 7041
N
P
scale 0 — 1 miles

Location
Lying at the southern tip of the peninsular south of Stranraer, the reserve is reached via the A716 road to Drummore then the minor road to the lighthouse and cliffs. NX/157304.

Tenure
Three-quarters of a mile of cliff is a reserve by agreement with the Commissioners of Northern Lighthouses.

Status
SSSI. Grade 1.

Warden
None present. Enquiries to RSPB Scottish Office (page 7).

Habitat
Rugged granite cliffs on the peninsular headland.

Birds
Nesting colonies of guillemot, razorbill, kittiwake, black guillemot, shag, cormorant, fulmar and both great black-backed and herring gulls. Manx shearwaters and gannets regularly pass the headland.

Other wildlife
Plants of the cliff-top include spring squill and purple milk vetch.

Visiting
Access at all times, but *visitors are warned not to go to the cliff-edge* which is dangerous.

Port Rodie, Stranraer, Dumfries and Galloway (tel: 0776 2595).

Nearest railway station
Stranraer (21 miles) on the line from Glasgow.

Black guillemot

North Hill, Papa Westray, Orkney

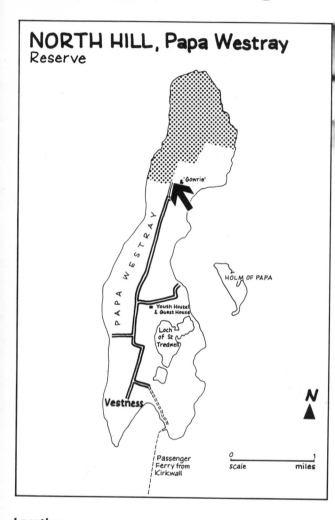

NORTH HILL, Papa Westray
Reserve

PAPA WESTRAY

'Gowrie'

HOLM OF PAPA

Youth Hostel & Guest House

Loch of St Tredwell

Vestness

Passenger Ferry from Kirkwall

0   scale   1   miles

N

Location
The reserve occupies the northern part of this small Orkney island with its entrance at the north end of the principal road. HY/496538.

Tenure
510 acres managed by agreement with the island's crofters.

Status
SSSI. Grade 1*.

Warden

Present from mid-April to mid-August, c/o Gowrie, Papa Westray KW17 2BU.

Habitat

A large maritime heath of sedge, heather, crowberry and creeping willow bordered by a rocky coastline with some low sandstone cliffs.

Birds

An exceptionally large colony of Arctic terns nest on the heath close to Arctic skua, eider, ringed plover, oystercatcher, dunlin, wheatear and four species of gulls. Several corncrakes still breed just off the reserve. Black guillemot, razorbill, guillemot, puffin, kittiwake, shag and rock dove inhabit the cliffs. Fowl Craig was one of the last great auk breeding sites in Britain. Several migrant species occur including some rarities.

Other wildlife

Scottish primrose, alpine meadow-rue, mountain everlasting and frog orchid are notable plants.

Visiting

Access at all times but visitors are asked to contact the summer warden on arrival, preferably having arranged in advance an escorted tour to view the nesting colonies. These may be viewed well from the perimeter path.

Facilities

G to Orkney Reserves 60p

Orkney Tourist Board, 6 Broad Street, Kirkwall (tel: 0856 2856).

Contact the Papa Community Co-op, Papa Westray, Orkney (tel: 085 74 267) for details of self-catering and guest house accommodation.

The island is reached by passenger **ferry** from Kirkwall or by **air service** from Kirkwall airport. Enquiries to Loganair (tel: 2494).

Eider

North Hoy, Orkney

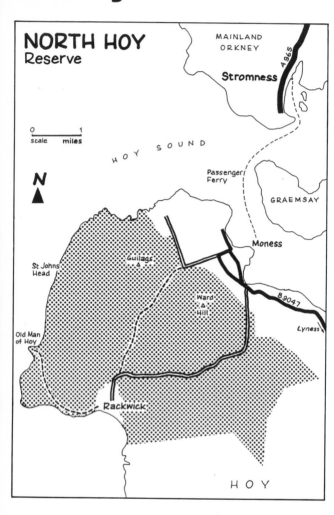

Location
Occupying the north-west part of the island of Hoy around Ward Hill, the reserve is reached either by passenger ferry from Stromness to Moness pier then a short walk to the reserve boundary (HY/223034), or by car ferry from Houton to Lyness then up the B9047 road to Rackwick (ND/203995).

Tenure
9,700 acres owned.

Status
SSSI. Grade 1.

Warden
Keith Fairclough, Ley House, North Hoy, Orkney.

Habitat
A large plateau of moorland, dissected by glacial valleys, and varying from heather and deer grass to mountain heath and sub-Arctic vegetation on the summit. The reserve also contains several miles of spectacular cliffs rising to 1,100ft at St John's Head.

Birds
Large populations of great and Arctic skuas breed on the moorland with red grouse, golden plover, dunlin, curlew, hen harrier, merlin, short-eared owl, twite and great black-backed gull. Guillemot, razorbill, kittiwake, shag, peregrine and raven nest on the cliffs with a colony of Manx shearwaters nearby.

Other wildlife
Alpine plants such as purple saxifrage, moss campion and Alpine saw-wort grow in the gullies and on ledges. Mountain hares are present.

Visiting
Access at all times, there being a footpath through the glen between Ward Hill and Guilags and another from the village of Rackwick to the famous Old Man of Hoy rock stack. Visitors are warned to *take special care* on the cliff-tops which are crumbly. There is an information display at the Hoy Inn at Moness.

Facilities
IC   **G** to Orkney Reserves 60p

Orkney Tourist Board, 6 Broad Street, Kirkwall (tel: 0856 2856).

There is a hostel in Rackwick and another ¾ mile along the road from Moness pier.

Taxis or hire-cars are available on the island — enquire at the pier. See also page 131.

Merlin

Noup Cliffs, Orkney

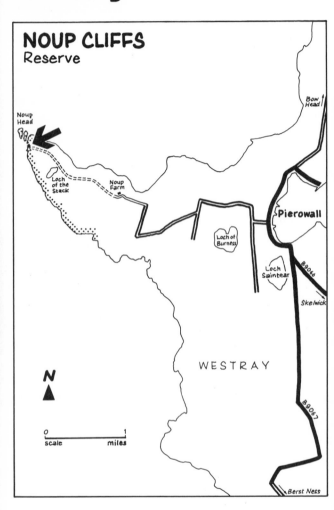

NOUP CLIFFS
Reserve

Bow Head

Noup Head

Loch of the Stack

Noup Farm

Pierowall

Loch of Burness

Loch Saintear

B9046

Skelwick

WESTRAY

N

B9067

0 — 1
scale — miles

Berst Ness

Location
Forming the western promontory of the island of Westray, the cliffs are approached from Pierowall along the minor road to Noup Farm then the track to the lighthouse at the north end of the reserve. HY/392500.

Tenure
1½ miles of cliff owned.

Status
SSSI. Grade 1*.

Warden
None present. Enquiries to RSPB Orkney Officer (page 7).

Habitat
High sandstone sea cliffs with numerous ledges and backed by maritime heath (off the reserve).

Birds
This is one of the largest seabird colonies in the British Isles with immense numbers of guillemots and kittiwakes, the other nesting species being razorbill, puffin, shag, fulmar, herring and great black-backed gulls, rock pipit and raven.

Other wildlife
Grey seals and occasionally porpoises and dolphins are seen offshore.

Visiting
Access at all times to the cliff-top (please *take great care*) from where excellent views may be obtained of the seabirds. Visitors are asked to close gates on the access track.

Facilities
G to Orkney Reserves 60p

Orkney Tourist Board, 6 Broad Street, Kirkwall (tel: 0856 2856).

B&B, self-catering and farmhouse accommodation are available on Westray.

The island is reached by passenger **ferry** from Kirkwall or by **air service** from Kirkwall airport. Enquiries to Loganair (tel: 2494).

Puffin

Trumland, Rousay, Orkney

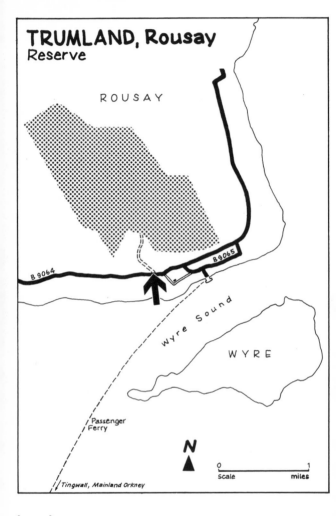

TRUMLAND, Rousay
Reserve

ROUSAY

B 9064

B 9065

Wyre Sound

WYRE

Passenger
Ferry

N

0   1
scale   miles

Tingwall, Mainland Orkney

Location
The reserve lies above Trumland House in the south of the island of Rousay which is reached by passenger ferry from Tingwall off the A966 road in the north-east of Mainland Orkney.

Tenure
1,070 acres owned.

Warden
Present from April to August at Trumland Mill Cottage, Rousay, Orkney. Otherwise enquiries to RSPB Orkney Officer (page 7).

Habitat

Mainly heather moorland rising to 800ft at Blotchnie Fiold, dissected by small valleys and containing a lochan and some crags known as 'hamars'.

Birds

Red-throated diver, hen harrier, kestrel and golden plover breed and short-eared owl, merlin and both great and Arctic skuas may be seen. A mixed colony of herring and lesser black-backed gulls is located on the moorland where both great black-backed and common gulls also nest.

Other wildlife

Orkney voles are present and otters visit the reserve occasionally.

Visiting

Access at all times, but visitors are asked to contact the summer warden who will escort them. A shop and public toilets are located in the village near the pier.

Facilities
WC

Orkney Tourist Board, 6 Broad Street, Kirkwall (tel: 0856 2856).

Some hotel and bed and breakfast accommodation is available on the island.

For details of **ferries** to Orkney see page 131.

Great skua

The Green Hotel

A well appointed privately owned hotel conveniently situated beside the M90 Edinburgh-Perth Motorway with many noted ornithological sites within an easy hour's drive.

The nearby Forth and Tay estuaries boast large populations of waders, seabird colonies abound on the islands in the Forth, and Ospreys usually nest at the SWT Reserve at Loch of the Lowes.

Kinross itself lies on the shores of Loch Leven, famous for its wildfowl – particularly grey geese in winter – the RSPB Vane Farm Nature Centre, and of course its superb trout fishing.

At the Green, the traditions of a warm welcome, fine food and ample accommodation, originating in the days when the hotel was a famous coaching inn, are still in evidence and today they are supplemented by a range of leisure facilities catering for almost every interest.

Write or phone for brochure and area guide and details of our special breaks.

2 The Muirs, Kinross, Tayside, KY13 7AS. Tel (0577) 63467.

Vane Farm, Tayside

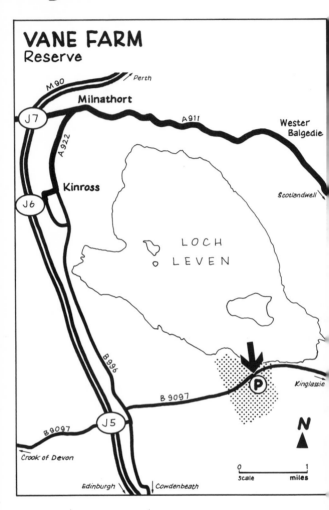

Location
Lying on the southern shore of Loch Leven east of Kinross, the reserve and nature centre are entered off the B9097 road to Glenrothes two miles east of junction 5 on the M90. NT/160991

Tenure
298 acres owned.

Status
SSSI.

Warden

Jim Stevenson, Vane Farm Nature Centre, Kinross KY13 7LX (tel: 0577 62355).

Habitat

A variety of habitats surround this educational nature centre which overlooks Loch Leven: marshy areas with shallow lagoons, mixed farmland and heather moorland with birch and bracken slopes and rocky outcrops.

Birds

Greylag geese occasionally graze the fields in winter when wigeon, teal, mallard, curlew, shoveler and whooper swan also occur. Large concentrations of pink-footed geese may then be watched over the loch with goosander, tufted duck and pochard. In summer gadwall, shelduck, great crested grebe and redshank frequent the 'scrape' while tree pipit, redpoll and willow warbler occupy the birchwoods.

Other wildlife

Primrose, wood sorrel, harebell and mountain pansy are some of the plants.

Visiting

Access at all times to the car park and nature trail. A hide overlooks the scrape. The nature centre with observation room and RSPB gift shop is open on all days from April to Christmas, 10.00am to 5.00pm, but on a limited basis from January to March. School parties are especially welcome by appointment.

Facilities

P   **IC**   **WC**   **S**   **G** 30p

Turfhills Service Area, M90, Kinross, Tayside (tel: 0577 63680).

See advertisement pages 182-183.

Nearest railway station

Lochgelly (5 miles) on the minor line from Edinburgh to Dundee.

Wood of Cree, Dumfries and Galloway

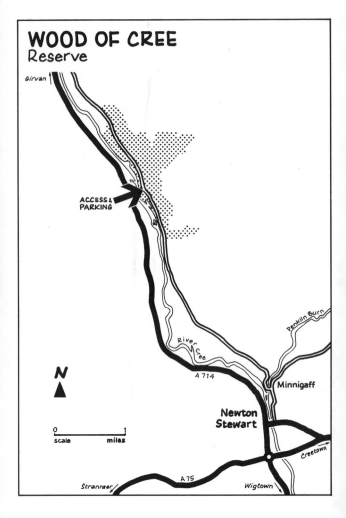

Location

Rising from the east bank of the River Cree four miles north-west of Newton Stewart, the reserve is approached on the minor road from Minnigaff running parallel to the A714. NX/382708.

Tenure

524 acres owned.

Status
SSSI. Grade 2.

Warden
Paul Collin, Gairland, Old Edinburgh Road, Minnigaff, Newton Stewart DG8 6PL.

Habitat
One of the largest broadleaved woods in the south of Scotland, consisting largely of old coppice of sessile oak, birch and hazel. Several burns tumble down through the wood from the moorland above to the riverside marsh.

Birds
Redstart, pied flycatcher, wood warbler, tree pipit, garden warbler, woodcock, great spotted woodpecker, buzzard and sparrowhawk breed in the woods. Common sandpiper, dipper and grey wagtail frequent the streams and mallard, teal and oystercatcher the riverside while curlew and whinchat are found on the moorland fringe.

Other wildlife
Roe deer and otters are present. Purple hairstreak and dark-green fritillary are among the butterflies. There is a rich bryophyte flora.

Visiting
Access at all times along a woodland track which leads up from the grassy roadside pull-off.

Dashwood Square, Newton Stewart, Dumfries and Galloway (tel: 0671 2431).

Nearest railway station
Dumfries, with a bus service connecting it to Newton Stewart (4 miles).

Woodcock

WALES

Coed Garth Gell, Gwynedd

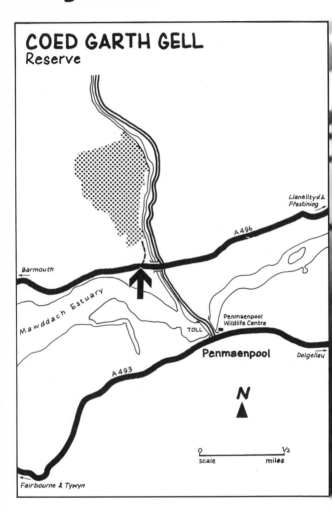

Location
Situated at the southern edge of Snowdonia National Park and overlooking the Mawddach estuary, the reserve is reached by walking up the public footpath from the A496 road from Barmouth to Dolgellau, starting nearly opposite the tollbridge road which crosses the estuary to Penmaenpool. SH/687191.

Tenure
114 acres owned.

Warden
Reg Thorpe, 2 Tan y Garth, Friog, Fairbourne LL38 2RJ.

Habitat

A sessile oak and birch wood with heather glades and a river gorge below the hills.

Birds

The breeding species include buzzard, raven, pied flycatcher, redstart, wood warbler, tree pipit, grey wagtail and all three species of woodpeckers.

Visiting

Access at all times along woodland paths. Cars should be parked in the lay-by on the A496. From late May to September the Penmaenpool Wildlife Centre, on the opposite side of the estuary, is open daily.

The Bridge, Dolgellau, Gwynedd (tel: 0341 422888).

See advertisement page 194.

Nearest railway station

Barmouth (7 miles) on the line from Shrewsbury to Pwllheli.

Buzzard

Cwm Clydach, West Glamorgan

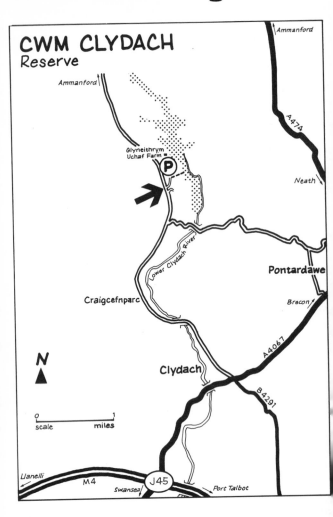

CWM CLYDACH
Reserve

Ammanford

Ammanford

A474

Glyneithrym
Uchaf Farm

P

Neath

Lower Clydach River

Pontardawe

Craigcefnparc

Brecon

N

A4067

Clydach

B4291

scale   miles

Llanelli   M4   J45   Port Talbot

Swansea

Location
Take the minor road up the river valley from Clydach which lies off
the A4067 road from Swansea north-east of its junction with the
M4. The reserve car park lies three miles north of Clydach, through
the village of Craigcefnparc, at Glyneithrym Uchaf Farm
SN/682053.

Tenure
22 acres leased and 98 acres managed by agreement with Lt Col
A D Holland.

Warden

Martin Humphreys, c/o Ty'r Wann, Craigcefnparc, Clydach, West Glamorgan.

Habitat

Oak woodland lining the banks of the lower River Clydach with smaller areas of birch and beech and wetter ground containing ash and alder. Heather and bracken slopes lie above the woodland.

Birds

Nesting buzzard, sparrowhawk and raven are frequently seen. Nestboxes are used by pied flycatcher, redstart and tits while wood warbler, all three species of woodpecker, nuthatch, treecreeper and tawny owl also nest in the woods. Dipper and grey wagtail frequent the river and tree pipit and wheatear the higher ground. Snipe, woodcock, redpoll and siskin are plentiful in winter.

Other wildlife

Badger and fox are present. The many species of butterflies include purple hairstreak and silver-washed fritillary.

Visiting

Access at all times to a waymarked path along the riverside. Visitors are asked to keep strictly to this footpath and to respect the rights of the farming tenants without whose co-operation the reserve could not have been established.

Facilities

P

i

Singleton Street, Swansea, West Glamorgan (tel: 0792 468321).

Nearest railway station

Swansea (10 miles) on the line from Cardiff.

Silver-washed fritillary

GLANRANNELL PARK HOTEL

RAC ★ ★
AA ★ ★

Crugybar, Llanwrda
Dyfed SA19 8SA
Telephone: Talley (055 83) 230

British Tourist Authority Commended Country House Hotel

PLEASE
SEND
FOR OUR
BROCHURE

Over the last fifteen years, Glanrannell has become well known to birdwatchers.

The hotel is a super centre to visit the many habitats of West Wales, RSPB reserves, sea cliffs, moorland and wetland and the lovely wooded valleys and hills that surround the hotel. The special birds of the area include pied flycatcher, redstart, raven, buzzard, wood warbler, peregrine and of course the red kite which still retains a stronghold in the valleys of West and Mid Wales, and is often seen soaring over the hotel.

Dinas and Gwenffrwd, Dyfed

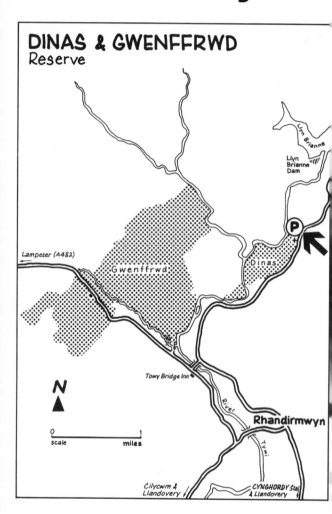

Location
Lying in the Tywi valley of the central Welsh hills, Dinas reserve is entered off the road to the Llyn Brianne dam north of Rhandirmwyn village. SN/788472. For access to the Gwenffrwd part of the reserve see below.

Tenure
1,700 acres owned.

Status
SSSI. Grade 1.

Warden

Tony Pickup, Troedrhiwgelynen, Rhandirmwyn, Llandovery SA20 0PN.

Habitat

Hillside oakwoods with rocky outcrops, streams and bracken slopes rising to heather and grass moorland with valley fields and riverside woodland.

Birds

Buzzard, sparrowhawk, kestrel, raven and red kite are seen in the neighbourhood, particularly in spring. Many woodland nestboxes are used by pied flycatchers, and other breeding birds include redstart, wood warbler, nuthatch, woodcock, tits and woodpeckers. Grey wagtail, common sandpiper and dipper frequent the rivers, tree pipit and whinchat the hillsides and wheatear and red grouse the moorland.

Other wildlife

Polecats are seen occasionally. Salmon and trout inhabit the river.

Visiting

The Dinas nature trail is accessible at all times from the car park where an Information Centre is open in summer. The terrain is rough and steep in places. For enjoyment of the two-three miles hill nature trails at the Gwenffrwd, starting by the warden's house, visitors are asked to report to the Dinas Information Centre.

Facilities

P   IC   G 30p

_i_

Central Car Park, Broad Street, Llandovery, Dyfed (tel: 0550 20693).

There are several camp and caravan sites in the upper Tywi valley.

See advertisements pages 194-195.

Nearest railway station

Cynghordy (9 miles) on the line from Shrewsbury to Swansea.

Dyffryn Wood, Powys

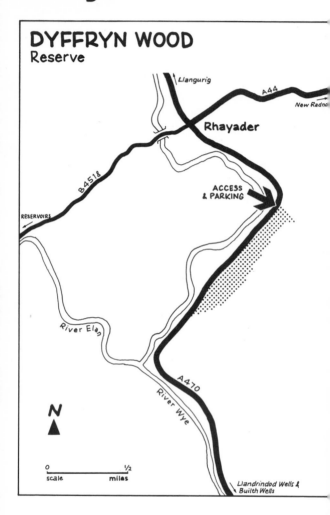

DYFFRYN WOOD
Reserve

Llangurig

A44

New Radnor

Rhayader

B4518

ACCESS & PARKING

RESERVOIRS

River Elan

A470

River Wye

N

0 scale ½ miles

Llandrindod Wells & Builth Wells

Location
Forming part of the composite RSPB reserve holding in the upper reaches of the River Wye and Elan, this wood lies beside the A470 road to Builth Wells just south of Rhayader.

Tenure
65 acres owned.

Warden
Richard Knight, c/o RSPB Wales Office (page 7).

Habitat
A hillside woodland predominantly of sessile oak.

Birds
Pied flycatcher, wood warbler and redstart breed plentifully with a few pairs of raven and buzzard, while grey wagtail and dipper nest along the streams. On the Corngafallt Common, part of the Wye/Elan reserve, are found whinchat, stonechat and red grouse and there is the possibility of seeing birds of prey such as red kite and peregrine.

Visiting
Access at all times to the woodland walk starting at the lay-by at the north end of the wood (SN/980672). The nearby Corngafallt Common is accessible along public footpaths from the minor road between Llanwrthwl and Elan village (SN/940641).

Elan Valley Visitor Centre, near Rhyader, Powys (tel: 0597 810898).

Nearest railway station
Llandrindod Wells (11 miles) on the line from Shrewsbury to Swansea.

Red kite

Grassholm, Dyfed

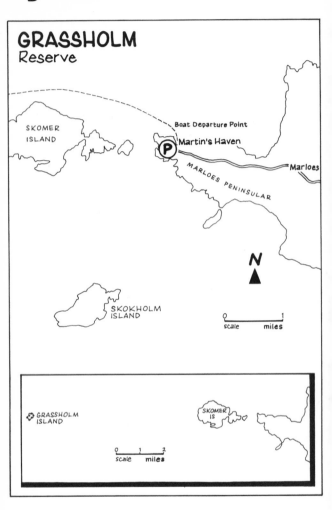

GRASSHOLM
Reserve

SKOMER ISLAND

Boat Departure Point

Martin's Haven

MARLOES PENINSULAR

Marloes

N

0 scale 1 miles

SKOKHOLM ISLAND

GRASSHOLM ISLAND

SKOMER IS

0 1 2 scale miles

Location
Lies ten miles off the coast of west Wales and beyond the other bird-rich Pembrokeshire islands of Skomer and Skokholm.

Tenure
22 acres owned.

Status
SSSI. Grade 1*.

Honorary warden
David Saunders, c/o West Wales Trust for Nature Conservation, 7 Market Street, Haverfordwest, Dyfed (tel: 5462).

Habitat
An isolated, rocky island rising to 150ft above sea level.

Birds
Grassholm is renowned for its immense breeding colony of gannets which numbered about 28,500 pairs in 1984, making this the second largest gannetry in the British Isles. There are also small numbers of guillemot, razorbill, shag, kittiwake, herring gull, great black-backed gull and oystercatcher. Manx shearwaters may be seen over the sea.

Visiting
The island is inaccessible except in very calm weather. Boat landings are permitted *only from 15 June onwards* so that the gannets are not disturbed while incubating their eggs. There is a boat service from Martinshaven (SM/761090) on the Marloes peninsular: further details from RSPB Wales Office (page 7). The gannets can be viewed well on the island from outside the sanctuary area which is demarcated by white posts.

Car Park, Broad Haven, Dyfed (tel: 043 783 412).

See advertisements pages 202 and 203.

Nearest railway station
Milford Haven (12 miles) on the line from Cardiff to Swansea.

Gannet

COASTAL COTTAGES OF PEMBROKESHIRE

We are greatly privileged to be able to offer, perhaps, the finest collection of Coastal holiday homes currently available in the United Kingdom. Our illustrated brochure, of over 150 properties, gives a fascinating insight into the unchanged world in this beautiful area. Many are of the highest possible residential standards, with Special Awards and full central heating, log fires, dishwashers and washing machines. All are close to sandy beaches along the more peaceful areas of the Pembrokeshire Coast. Some have Heron, Badgers or Foxes close by; even a colony of seals. Many have sea views and stunning sunsets.

All properties are sensibly priced to give excellent value at prices ranging from £155 to £525 high-season and £50 to £95 low-season. Available all year. Pets welcome at most properties. A.A. Recommended and W.T.B. Approval.

TELEPHONE 03483 7742
ABERCASTLE, PEMBROKESHIRE
SA62 5HJ

Lake Vyrnwy, Powys

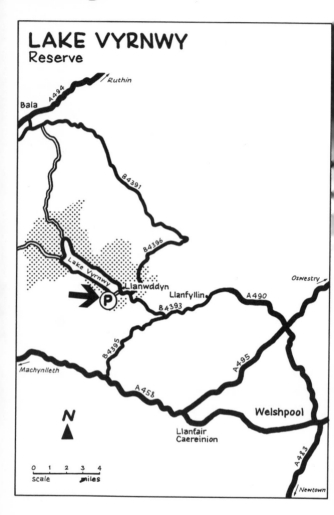

Location
This reservoir lies in the Berwyn hills west of Llanfyllin from where the reserve information centre by the dam is reached via the B4393 road to Llanwddyn. SJ/020193.

Tenure
1,320 acres owned and 16,200 acres of the water catchment managed for conservation by agreement with the Severn Trent Water Authority.

Status
Mostly SSSI. Grade 1.

Warden

Mike Walker, Bryn Awel, Llanwddyn, Oswestry, Salop.

Habitat

Extensive heather moorland with conifer plantations, mixed deciduous woodland and sessile oakwoods, meadows and rocky streams surrounding Lake Vyrnwy reservoir.

Birds

Goosander, grey wagtail, common sandpiper, dipper and kingfisher nest by the lake and rocky streams. The mixed deciduous woodland contains nuthatch, treecreeper, sparrowhawk, chiffchaff, garden warbler and both green and great spotted woodpeckers, while the sessile oakwoods are favoured by redstart, wood warbler and pied flycatcher. Crossbill and siskin nest in the conifers. Raven, buzzard, merlin and hen harrier frequent the moorland where wheatear, ring ouzel, curlew and golden plover breed.

Other wildlife

Red squirrels and polecats are present. The many species of butterflies include small pearl-bordered and highbrown fritillaries with large heath on the moorland.

Visiting

Visitors may travel round the reservoir by car. There are paths which may be walked, as well as a hide by the north-west shore. Two woodland nature trails, including a hide, are accessible at all times, and there is another hide suitable for wheelchairs. The Information Centre, in the old chapel is open during most hours of the summer.

Facilities

P   **WC**   **IC**   ♿   **G** 30p

Oswestry Library, Arthur Street, Oswestry, Salop (tel: 0691 662753).

See advertisement page 194.

Nearest railway station

Welshpool (21 miles) on the line from Shrewsbury to Aberystwyth.

Point of Air, Clwyd

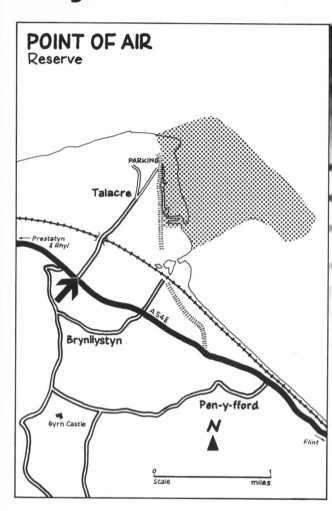

POINT OF AIR
Reserve

PARKING

Talacre

← Prestatyn & Rhyl

Brynllystyn

A548

Pen-y-fford

Gyrn Castle

N

Flint

0 1
Scale   miles

Location
Lying at the mouth of the Dee estuary on the Welsh side, a vantage point for this reserve is located at the end of Station Road, Talacre, which is reached off the coastal A548 road two miles east of Prestatyn. SJ/113833.

Tenure
600 acres held by agreement with two owners.

Status
SSSI. Grade 1*.

Warden
None present. Enquiries to RSPB Wales Office (page 7).

Habitat
Inter-tidal mudflats with a shingle spit and a small area of saltmarsh.

Birds
Up to 20,000 waders roost here in winter, particularly oyster-catcher, knot, dunlin and redshank, while ringed plover and sanderling occur on migration. Mallard, shelduck, teal, wigeon, pintail and red-breasted merganser also winter when snow bunting, twite and occasionally Lapland bunting and shorelark frequent the shingle spit. Several species of terns occur in summer.

Visiting
Access at all times, with limited car parking space on the *landward* side only of the sea wall. Visitors are asked not to disturb roosting waders and should not go onto the mudflats when the tide is rising.

Council Offices, Nant Hall Road, Prestatyn, Clywd (tel: 074 56 2484).

Nearest railway station
Prestatyn (2 miles) on the main line from Crewe to Holyhead.

Shelduck

South Stack Cliffs, Gwynedd

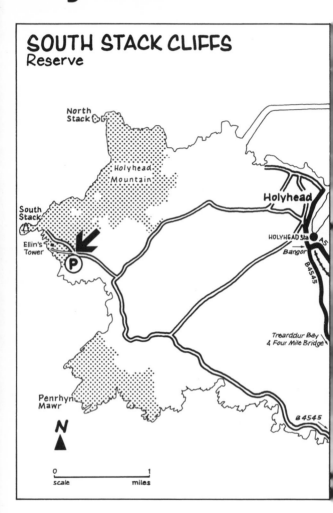

Location
Forming the western headland of Anglesey, the cliffs are sign-posted by road from the town of Holyhead. SH/207821.

Tenure
780 acres leased from Anglesey Borough Council.

Status
SSSI. Grade 1.

Warden
Present from April to August at Plas Nico, South Stack, Holyhead, Anglesey.

Habitat
High cliffs with caves and offshore stacks, backed by the maritime heathland of Holyhead Mountain.

Birds
Several pairs of choughs occupy these cliffs whose ledges are used by thousands of guillemot, razorbill and kittiwake as well as several puffins. Raven, jackdaw, shag and one or two pairs of peregrine also nest here, with stonechat and whitethroat on the heath. Manx shearwaters and gannets pass offshore and sometimes unusual species like pomarine skua.

Other wildlife
Marsh fritillary and silver-studded blue butterflies occur. The cliff-tops are colourful in the spring with thrift and spring squill, and spotted rock rose is a speciality.

Visiting
Access at all times to the car park from where a short track leads to Ellin's Tower, the information centre with a panoramic view of the cliffs and seabirds. Other car parks are also available.

Facilities
P   **WC**   **IC**   **G** 30p

Marine Square, Salt Island Approach, Holyhead, Gwynedd (tel: 0407 2622).

Nearest railway station
Holyhead (3¼ miles) on the main line from Crewe.

Stonechat

Ynys-Hir, Dyfed

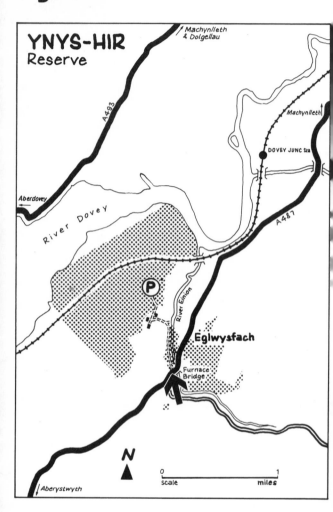

YNYS-HIR Reserve

Machynlleth & Dolgellau

A493

Machynlleth

Aberdovey

River Dovey

DOVEY JUNC Sta

A487

P

River Einion

Eglwysfach

Furnace Bridge

N

Aberystwyth

0   1
scale   miles

Location
Lying at the head of the Dyfi estuary, this reserve is entered from the A487 road from Machynlleth to Aberystwyth at the village of Furnace. SN/685952.

Tenure
661 acres owned.

Status
SSSI. Grade 1.

Warden

Dick Squires, Cae'r Berllan, Eglwysfach, Machynlleth, Powys SY20 8TA.

Habitat

The grazed saltmarsh of the Dyfi estuary is bordered by freshwater marsh and some remnant peat bogs. Mixed deciduous and conifer woodlands, with a river gorge, rise to a rocky hillside with bracken slopes.

Birds

The oakwoods contain pied flycatcher, redstart, wood warbler, nuthatch, great and blue tits and both great spotted and lesser spotted woodpeckers. Goldcrest and coal tit prefer the conifers and sedge and grasshopper warblers the marshland. Buzzard, kestrel and sparrowhawk breed in the woods while red-breasted merganser and common sandpiper frequent the river. Peregrine, merlin and hen harrier hunt over the reserve outside the breeding season. Wintering wildfowl include wigeon, mallard, teal and a small flock of Greenland white-fronted geese.

Other wildlife

Sundew, bog rosemary and bog asphodel grow in the bogs. Many butterfly species include dark green fritillary. Badgers and polecats occur.

Visiting

Open on all days from 9.00am to 9.00pm or sunset when earlier. A nature trail starts from the information centre, with toilets, and a number of hides are positioned by the estuary and marsh. Another is elevated in the woodland canopy. Charge: £2 to non-members.

Facilities

P   **WC**   **IC**   **G** 30p

Eastgate, Aberystwyth, Dyfed (tel: 0970 612125).

See advertisements on page 212.

Nearest railway station

Dovey Junction (3 miles) on the line from Shrewsbury to Aberystwyth.

NORTHERN IRELAND

Castlecaldwell Forest, Co Fermanagh

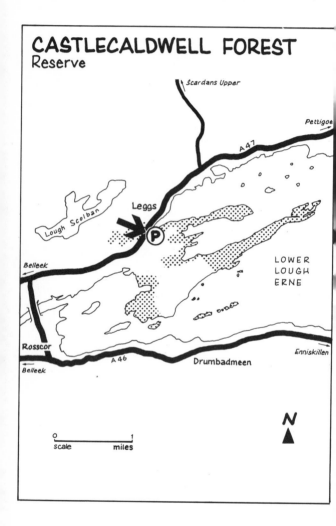

CASTLECALDWELL FOREST
Reserve

Location
Lying on the west side of Lower Lough Erne, this peninsular is entered off the A47 road to Pettigoe four miles east of Belleek. H/009603.

Tenure
37 acres of islands owned while 554 acres of the forest are managed by agreement with the Northern Ireland Forest Service.

Warden
Joe Magee, Castlecaldwell, Leggs PO, Co Fermanagh.

Habitat
Predominantly a conifer forest fringed by bays of the lough with willow and alder scrub and reedbeds. The reserve also incorporates several low islands in the lough.

Birds
Of principal importance for the population of common scoters which nest on the vegetated islands with mallard, tufted duck, red-breasted merganser and heron, while common and Sandwich terns with black-headed gulls use the barer ones. Sparrowhawk, long-eared owl and siskin inhabit the forest and both great crested and little grebes the bays. Corncrakes breed in the vicinity. Wigeon, goldeneye, teal, pochard, tufted duck and whooper swan occur in winter.

Visiting
Access at all times to the shoreline paths and a hide in Castle Bay. There is an information centre with toilets. School parties are welcome by appointment. Boat trips can be arranged with the warden.

Facilities
P   IC   WC

Lakeland Visitor Centre, Shore Road, Enniskillen, Co Fermanagh (tel: 0365 23110).

Sandwich tern

Green Island & Greencastle Point, Co Down

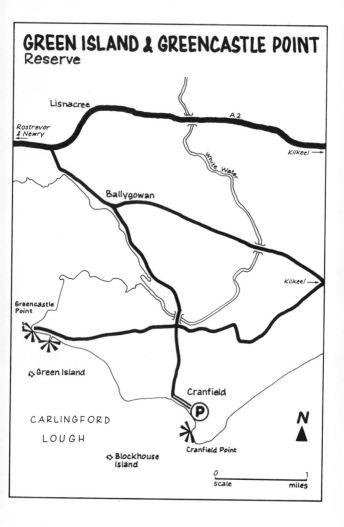

GREEN ISLAND & GREENCASTLE POINT
Reserve

Lisnacree

A 2

Rostrevor & Newry

Kilkeel →

White Water

Ballygowan

Kilkeel →

Greencastle Point

Green Island

Cranfield

P

CARLINGFORD

LOUGH

Cranfield Point

Blockhouse Island

N

0 scale 1 miles

Location
A promontory in the north-east of Carlingford Lough five miles south-west of Kilkeel. J/241118.

Tenure
2 acres leased from the National Trust and another owner.

Status
Green Island is an Area of Scientific Interest.

Warden
Dave Allen, 7 Loughermore Road, Ballykelly, Co Londonderry.

Habitat
Both Greencastle Point and the offshore Green Island (part of the reserve) are small rocky islets.

Birds
Important breeding colonies of roseate, common, Arctic and Sandwich terns with a few oystercatchers and ringed plovers.

Visiting
Good views of the terns may be obtained from the coast road at Greencastle. Access to the islets is strictly *prohibited* to avoid disturbing the nesting birds. Black guillemots nest at the nearby Cranfield Point lighthouse.

Caravan, Town Centre, Kilkeel, Co Down (tel: 069 37 63092).

Roseate tern

Lough Foyle, Co Londonderry

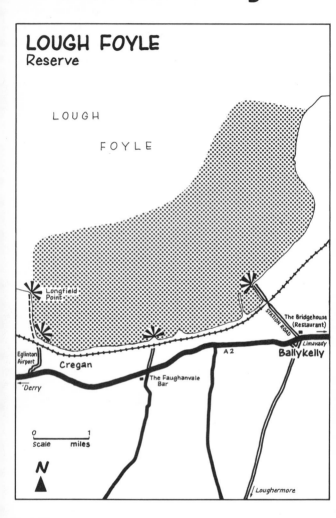

Location

The reserve embraces the south-east foreshore of Lough Foyle between Longfield Point almost to the Roe estuary.

Tenure

3,300 acres leased from the Crown Estate Commissioners.

Status

Area of Scientific Interest.

Warden
Dave Allen, 7 Loughermore Road, Ballykelly, Co Londonderry.

Habitat
Wide mudflats with a fringe of saltmarsh, shingle and shell ridges bordered by arable farmland (not within the reserve).

Birds
Lough Foyle is outstanding for its wintering wildfowl including thousands of wigeon, mallard, teal and pale-bellied brent geese with oystercatcher, dunlin, bar-tailed godwit, grey plover and curlew. Over 1,000 whooper swans feed on the adjacent farmland with Bewick's swans and white-fronted geese. Many snow buntings forage on the shore in winter. Whimbrel, Slavonian grebe, curlew, sandpiper, little stint and spotted redshank are some of the passage migrants.

Visiting
Access at all times to good viewpoints at Longfield Point, Ballykelly and Faughanvale, reached by taking minor roads off the main Limavady-Londonderry road, *taking care at the unmanned railway crossings.* Visitors are asked not to disturb the flocks of waders and wildfowl.

Facilities

7 Connell Street, Limavady, Co Londonderry (tel: 050 472 62226).

Nearest railway station
Londonderry (1 mile) on the line from Belfast.

Bewick's swan

Rathlin Island Cliffs, Co Antrim

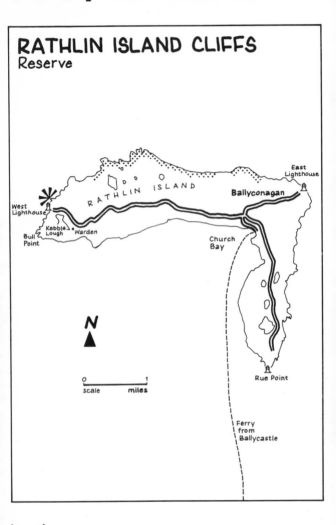

RATHLIN ISLAND CLIFFS
Reserve

East Lighthouse

West Lighthouse

Ballyconagan

RATHLIN ISLAND

Kebble Lough · Warden

Bull Point

Church Bay

N

0 scale 1 miles

Rue Point

Ferry from Ballycastle

Location
The island lies five miles across Rathlin Sound and is reached by local boat service from Ballycastle on the north Antrim coast.

Tenure
2½ miles of the island's northern cliffs owned.

Status
Kebble Nature Reserve is an Area of Scientific Interest.

Warden
Present from April to August at Kebble, Rathlin Island, Ballycastle, Co Antrim.

Habitat
The RSPB reserve comprises a stretch of basalt cliffs, some high and steep, others with grassy slopes above boulder beaches. The Society also wardens the Kebble Nature Reserve of the Department of Environment (Northern Ireland) which includes seacliffs at the western end of the island.

Birds
Large numbers of guillemot, razorbill, puffin, black guillemot, fulmar, shag, kittiwake and both great and lesser black-back gulls nest on the Kebble cliffs with stonechat, rock pipit and wheatear in the vicinity. Manx shearwaters nest above the northern cliffs where, as elsewhere on the island, buzzard, peregrine, raven and chough may be encountered. Gannets, skuas and occasionally petrels and sooty shearwaters pass offshore.

Other wildlife
Limestone bugle, spring squill and several species of orchids flower on the cliffs.

Visiting
Access at all times to the cliffs and footpaths. The seabird colony can be viewed well from beside the Kebble lighthouse (D/093516). Auks and shearwaters may be seen during the boat crossing to the island.

7 Mary Street, Ballycastle, Co Antrim (tel: 026 57 62024).

There are guest houses and caravans in Church Bay.

Nearest railway station
Ballymoney (15 miles) on the line from Belfast.
There is an irregular **minibus service** across the island to Kebble.

Puffin

Shanes Castle, Co Antrim

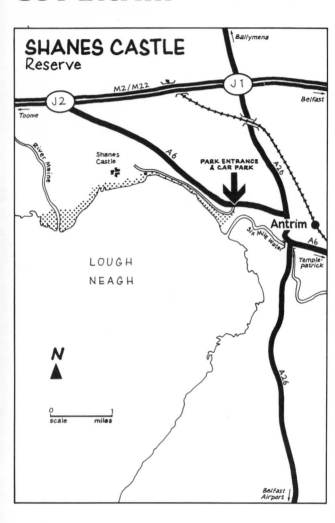

SHANES CASTLE
Reserve

Location
Forming part of an estate which is open to the public, the reserve lies beside Lough Neagh and is entered from the Randalstown Road ¼ mile from Antrim. J/136874.

Tenure
88 acres leased from the Lord O'Neill.

Status
Area of Scientific Interest.

Warden
Eddie Franklin, 67 Greenview Avenue, Co Antrim (tel: 084 94 63238).

Habitat
Mixed woodland and parkland on the shore of Lough Neagh where there is also some marsh with alder and willow scrub.

Birds
Heron, kingfisher, great crested grebe, teal, shelduck, long-eared owl, sparrowhawk, buzzard, blackcap and magpie nest here. Large flocks of mallard, teal, pochard, tufted duck, goldeneye, coot with some Bewick's swans and greylag geese winter on the lough.

Other wildlife
Red squirrel, badger and fallow deer occur. The plants include heath spotted orchid, adder's tongue and broad-leaved helleborine.

Visiting
The reserve is accessible during the times (reviewed each year) when the estate is open to the public, but otherwise by arrangement with the warden. There is a nature trail with a hide overlooking a bay of the lough. The estate operates a steam railway which runs through the park to the Castle as well as a café, toilets and funfair.

Facilities
P

43 Queen's Avenue, Magherafelt, Co Londonderry (tel: 0648 32151).

Nearest railway station
Antrim (¼ mile) on the line from Belfast.

Teal

Bird checklist

Species	Date	Reserve
Red-throated Diver		
Black-throated Diver		
Great Northern Diver		
Little Grebe		
Great Crested Grebe		
Red-necked Grebe		
Slavonian Grebe		
Black-necked Grebe		
Fulmar		
Cory's Shearwater		
Great Shearwater		
Sooty Shearwater		
Manx Shearwater		
Storm Petrel		
Leach's Petrel		
Gannet		
Cormorant		
Shag		
Bittern		
Grey Heron		
Purple Heron		
White Stork		
Spoonbill		
Mute Swan		
Bewick's Swan		
Whooper Swan		
Bean Goose		
Pink-footed Goose		

Bird checklist

Species	Date	Reserve
White-fronted Goose		
Greylag Goose		
Snow Goose		
Canada Goose		
Barnacle Goose		
Brent Goose		
Egyptian Goose		
Shelduck		
Mandarin		
Wigeon		
Gadwall		
Teal		
Mallard		
Pintail		
Garganey		
Shoveler		
Red-crested Pochard		
Pochard		
Ferruginous Duck		
Tufted Duck		
Scaup		
Eider		
Long-tailed Duck		
Common Scoter		
Velvet Scoter		
Goldeneye		
Smew		
Red-breasted Merganser		

Bird checklist		
Species	**Date**	**Reserve**
Goosander		
Ruddy Duck		
Honey Buzzard		
Red Kite		
Marsh Harrier		
Hen Harrier		
Montagu's Harrier		
Goshawk		
Sparrowhawk		
Buzzard		
Rough-legged Buzzard		
Golden Eagle		
Osprey		
Kestrel		
Merlin		
Hobby		
Peregrine		
Red Grouse		
Ptarmigan		
Black Grouse		
Capercaillie		
Red-legged Partridge		
Grey Partridge		
Quail		
Pheasant		
Golden Pheasant		
Lady Amherst's Pheasant		
Water Rail		

Bird checklist		
Species	**Date**	**Reserve**
Spotted Crake		
Corncrake		
Moorhen		
Coot		
Oystercatcher		
Avocet		
Stone Curlew		
Little Ringed Plover		
Ringed Plover		
Kentish Plover		
Dotterel		
Golden Plover		
Grey Plover		
Lapwing		
Knot		
Sanderling		
Little Stint		
Temminck's Stint		
Pectoral Sandpiper		
Curlew Sandpiper		
Purple Sandpiper		
Dunlin		
Buff-breasted Sandpiper		
Ruff		
Jack Snipe		
Snipe		
Woodcock		
Black-tailed Godwit		

Bird checklist		
Species	**Date**	**Reserve**
Bar-tailed Godwit		
Whimbrel		
Curlew		
Spotted Redshank		
Redshank		
Greenshank		
Green Sandpiper		
Wood Sandpiper		
Common Sandpiper		
Turnstone		
Red-necked Phalarope		
Grey Phalarope		
Pomarine Skua		
Arctic Skua		
Long-tailed Skua		
Great Skua		
Mediterranean Gull		
Little Gull		
Sabine's Gull		
Black-headed Gull		
Common Gull		
Lesser Black-backed Gull		
Herring Gull		
Iceland Gull		
Glaucous Gull		
Great Black-backed Gull		
Kittiwake		
Sandwich Tern		

Bird checklist		
Species	Date	Reserve
Roseate Tern		
Common Tern		
Arctic Tern		
Little Tern		
Black Tern		
Guillemot		
Razorbill		
Black Guillemot		
Little Auk		
Puffin		
Rock Dove		
Stock Dove		
Woodpigeon		
Collared Dove		
Turtle Dove		
Cuckoo		
Barn Owl		
Little Owl		
Tawny Owl		
Long-eared Owl		
Short-eared Owl		
Nightjar		
Swift		
Kingfisher		
Hoopoe		
Wryneck		
Green Woodpecker		
Great Spotted Woodpecker		

Bird checklist		
Species	**Date**	**Reserve**
Lesser Spotted Woodpecker		
Woodlark		
Skylark		
Shore Lark		
Sand Martin		
Swallow		
House Martin		
Richard's Pipit		
Tawny Pipit		
Tree Pipit		
Meadow Pipit		
Rock Pipit		
Yellow Wagtail		
Grey Wagtail		
Pied Wagtail		
Waxwing		
Dipper		
Wren		
Dunnock		
Robin		
Nightingale		
Bluethroat		
Black Redstart		
Redstart		
Whinchat		
Stonechat		
Wheatear		
Ring Ouzel		

Bird checklist

Species	Date	Reserve
Blackbird		
Fieldfare		
Song Thrush		
Redwing		
Mistle Thrush		
Cetti's Warbler		
Grasshopper Warbler		
Savi's Warbler		
Aquatic Warbler		
Sedge Warbler		
Marsh Warbler		
Reed Warbler		
Icterine Warbler		
Melodious Warbler		
Dartford Warbler		
Barred Warbler		
Lesser Whitethroat		
Whitethroat		
Garden Warbler		
Blackcap		
Yellow-browed Warbler		
Wood Warbler		
Chiffchaff		
Willow Warbler		
Goldcrest		
Firecrest		
Spotted Flycatcher		
Red-breasted Flycatcher		

Bird checklist

Species	Date	Reserve
Pied Flycatcher		
Bearded Tit		
Long-tailed Tit		
Marsh Tit		
Willow Tit		
Crested Tit		
Coal Tit		
Blue Tit		
Great Tit		
Nuthatch		
Treecreeper		
Golden Oriole		
Red-backed Shrike		
Great Grey Shrike		
Jay		
Magpie		
Chough		
Jackdaw		
Rook		
Carrion/Hooded Crow		
Raven		
Starling		
House Sparrow		
Tree Sparrow		
Chaffinch		
Brambling		
Serin		
Greenfinch		

Bird checklist

Species	Date	Reserve
Goldfinch		
Siskin		
Linnet		
Twite		
Redpoll		
Common Crossbill		
Scottish Crossbill		
Scarlet Rosefinch		
Bullfinch		
Hawfinch		
Lapland Bunting		
Snow Bunting		
Yellowhammer		
Cirl Bunting		
Ortolan Bunting		
Reed Bunting		
Corn Bunting		

Index to Reserves

Scotland

Wales

Northern Ireland

The Royal Society for the Protection of Birds is one of the world's leading nature conservation organisations. With a fast-growing membership, its aim is to encourage conservation of wild birds by developing public interest in their beauty and place in nature. As well as the management of some 120 reserves, the Society's work includes scientific research, enforcement of protection laws, and education including film production, publishing and the running of the Young Ornithologists' Club for young people under the age of 15.

RSPB books

'What's that bird?'
by Peter Hayman and Michael Everett, £8·95
An invaluable guide to how birds look and behave in the field.
Peter Hayman's illustrations demonstrate how different birds fly,
move and feed. Michael Everett's comments tell you exactly what
points and marks to look for.

Drawing Birds, an RSPB Guide
by John Busby, £12·95
John Busby looks at birds with the eye of a birdwatcher and artist,
and explains his techniques with the ease and enthusiasm of the
expert teacher. For budding bird artists, this is essential reading,
and if you want to improve your field sketches, *Drawing Birds* will
be a revelation.

The RSPB Puzzle and Project Book
£3·95 paperback
From quick quizzes to tests of bird identification skills, this book is
full of mind-boggling puzzles, and has lots of exciting projects and
surveys to make birdwatching even more fun for all the family!

A Year of Bird Life
£4·95
A bright, colourful little book, full of facts and information about
birds for each month of the year. Ideal for younger members of the
family.

The above titles are available from the Sales Department, Royal
Society for the Protection of Birds, The Lodge, Sandy, Bedfordshire
SG19 2DL (plus postage and packing) and from all good
bookshops.

We should like to thank the advertisers in this edition of RSPB Reserves Visiting for their support; especially Corporate Members of the Society: Lochside Hotel, Red House Hotel, British Gas, Castle Head Field Centre, The Blakeney Hotel, Cambrian Bird Holidays, Flaneburg Hotel, Lasswade House Hotel, Bikerhyd Farm, Millmead Country Guest House, Glanrannel Park Hotel, White Horse Hotel, Barn Owl Travel, Shelbrooke Hotel, Fairlight Hotel, Oakdale House Hotel.

For full advertising details of the RSPB's magazine, *Birds*, please contact the Publications Department, Royal Society for the Protection of Birds, The Lodge, Sandy, Bedfordshire SG19 2DL.